businessbuddies

successful
leadership
skills

businessbuddies

successful
leadership
skills

Ken Lawson, M.A., Ed.M.

First edition for the United States, its territories and dependencies, and Canada
published 2006 by Barron's Educational Series, Inc.

Conceived and created by
Axis Publishing Limited
8c Accommodation Road
London NW11 8ED
www.axispublishing.co.uk

Creative Director: Siân Keogh
Editorial Director: Anne Yelland
Design: Sean Keogh, Simon de Lotz
Managing Editor: Conor Kilgallon
Production: Jo Ryan, Cécile Lerbière

NOTE: The opinions and advice expressed in this book are intended as a guide only. The publisher
and author accept no responsibility for any loss sustained as a result of using this book.

All inquiries should be addressed to:
Barron's Educational Series, Inc.
250 Wireless Boulevard
Hauppauge, New York 11788
www.barronseduc.com

Library of Congress Control No: 2004116960

ISBN-13: 978-0-7641-3246-9
ISBN-10: 0-7641-3246-6

Printed and bound in China
9 8 7 6 5 4 3 2 1

contents

Introduction   6

1 The skills of leadership   10

2 What type of leader are you?   54

3 Self-analysis   78

4 Situational analysis & team building   120

5 Motivation & communication   170

6 Evaluation & maintenance   202

Index   236

6

Introduction

Who comes to mind when you think about outstanding leaders? Many people think of Franklin D. Roosevelt or Winston Churchill. Do you think of Mahatma Gandhi? What about Rudolph Giuliani? Maybe you identify with IT visionaries like Bill Gates and Steve Jobs. Perhaps Donald J. Trump is on your list.

Whoever comes to your mind when you think about leadership, there's very little doubt about the qualities outstanding leaders share. They get things done. They motivate, they inspire, they move and shake, and they have an impact on how we work and live. In short, they set the pace for our everyday experience.

Successful Leadership Skills shows what it takes to be an outstanding leader and helps you understand why great leaders are made and not born. If you're new to the field of leadership, this book will give you ideas about how leaders behave. If you simply want to understand the qualities it takes to lead others, his book will show you. And if you're in a position to become a leader, this book will provide the heads-up you may need to hit the ground running.

Whether you lead in politics, business, or the arts, this book gets straight to the point and looks closely at the skills of leadership. You'll learn about the importance of credibility; taking initiative; experimenting and risk-taking; planning and innovation. You'll understand the value of big-picture thinking, questioning the status quo, and breaking the mold to blaze new trails.

You'll also learn about key leadership styles, and how they compare and contrast. Which style does your boss have? What will be your style? Can you take on different leadership styles in different situations and contexts? Will you want to?

This book offers insights into the qualities and attributes of outstanding leaders. You'll see what it takes to influence others, and how great leaders use

Introduction continued

their gifts and acquired abilities to sway others. You'll learn about team building, motivation, and the collaborative spirit. You'll see why effective leadership is the key to achievement in personal and organizational terms. And you'll understand why effective leaders go out of their way to develop the skills and abilities of the people they lead.

Successful Leadership Skills offers valuable tips and guidelines on motivating others, delegating work, and obtaining and listening to feedback. It will show you how to communicate as leaders do, and how to wear the mantle of leadership in the company of those you are leading. You'll also learn about developing networks, getting and giving recognition, and dealing with the stress that often accompanies the execution of leadership.

Outstanding leaders are not passive individuals. They are initiators, and doers. They raise their hands and they stand up to be seen. They are often great planners and nearly always full of purpose. They have a clear idea of what needs to get done. And they get it done. If you want to know how that happens, what it takes and where to begin, *Successful Leadership Skills* is for you. It's an absorbing read and is filled with practical ideas and resources to help you take charge of others comfortably and confidently. Go for it . . .

Ken Lawson, M.A., Ed.M.

Career management counselor and author

Instructor, School of Continuing and Professional Studies

New York University

1

the skills of leadership

Defining the task

Even leaders operate within a framework that has been laid down by others—their own superiors or the shareholders, for example. However, the key to the leadership role is knowing where they want to take their team and how to set goals and objectives in order to get them there.

ORGANIZATIONAL GOALS

Every organization has clear overall goals. These might include:

1 Engaging in continuous research and development to ensure an innovative range of products.

2 Achieving a defined percentage market share within a given time frame.

3 Reaching a financial turnover figure in a defined time frame.

4 Establishing a stock market flotation.

5 Making a profit or defined return on investment.

6 Penetrating foreign markets.

7 Working ethically, or for the common good.

8 Establishing market domination in one or more areas.

9 Growing the enterprise to employ a predetermined number of people.

Defining the task continued

The application and types of task drawn from these goals depends in large part on the level within an organization at which the individual leader works.

1 THE BOARD LEVEL
In a hierarchy, the board, or directors, and CEO are likely to be concerned with the overall objectives of the organization, whether that is profit or turnover related or moving into a foreign market. This might be termed the organization's mission.

2 SENIOR MANAGEMENT LEVEL
Senior managers will also be concerned with the organization's mission, but their remit will also include long-term, strategic objectives. The board might decide that they want turnover in five years time to be $1 million, the senior managers' job is to make that happen.

3 MIDDLE MANAGEMENT LEVEL
Some middle managers might be part of the process of "making it happen," but their main role is to ensure that the individual divisions they lead contribute to the long-term goal, as defined to them by senior management.

4 JUNIOR MANAGEMENT LEVEL

Those on the first rung on the management ladder, likely with support from middle management, make sure that departments or units work toward making the organizational goal a reality. They also motivate the individuals they lead, at a personal level, to perform effectively.

At each level in the chain of command, it is essential that leaders understand their tasks, and effectively convey to their subordinates where their key areas of responsibility lie, and what is expected of them, in order to achieve the goals of the organization.

In autocratic organizations, the chain of command often runs from the top down; in more democratic organizations, it may run from the bottom up. The thinking behind this is that if junior and middle managers set their own goals and targets, they will be more motivated to reach or exceed them. In fact, it is often more effective if a combination of these approaches is adopted.

Planning

The foundation of effective leadership is a plan. Planning can be divided into three elements: purpose, structure, and process.

PURPOSE

- At the heart of planning is the recognition that planning comes before all other management and leadership functions.

- Planning must also contribute to the overall goals of the organization and at the same time, offer clear and attainable objectives to those charged with implementing the plan.

- Part of the purpose of a plan is that it should clearly demonstrate the intended use of human and financial resources in an efficient and effective manner.

STRUCTURE

- If the planning process within an organization is structured and agreed upon, and all plans conform to the structure, the unification created makes implementing plans simpler.

- A corollary to this point is that, once a unified planning system has been seen to work effectively, the first option for managers will be to use this tried and tested procedure.

PROCESS

- Plans need a measure of flexibility to cope with changing market forces or changing personnel. A plan without flexibility might have to be abandoned if circumstances change; one with flexibility can be adapted.

- In addition, plans need a time frame within which they will be implemented. This time frame should be long enough to see if it is working, but not so long that circumstances have changed so dramatically that the plan is unlikely to succeed.

- The planning process must also take into account any factors that might limit—or that are crucial—to the likelihood of its successful implementation.

- The more these factors are accurately identified, the greater the likelihood that the most effective plan of action will be selected.

the skills of leadership

Initiative

Leaders make things happen; they motivate others to excel. They cannot do this by sitting back waiting for something to happen. A major quality of an effective leader is the desire and ability to take initiative.

PERSONAL INITIATIVE

When faced with opposition, or in uncertain or difficult circumstances, effective leaders are proactive. They positively embrace change, manage the process of change, and set up systems in which other people can act for the common good.

Proactive people:
- Try harder than others
- Do not give up easily
- See opportunity where others do not
- Find some good in an apparently bad situation or experience

Their personal activity and success will then "trickle down" through an organization. No one follows a leader who does not have the enthusiasm and drive to challenge the status quo.

FOSTERING INITIATIVE IN OTHERS

When people understand that their views will be listened to, that their contribution will be valued, and that any criticisms voiced over their actions will be constructive, they are motivated to act.

An effective leader knows when to initiate training programs, for example, so that when the time is right, his staff members have all the skills they need to contribute still further to the organization's goals and successes.

An organizational culture that challenges staff, while giving them the skills they need to meet new challenges and excel at them, is one in which there are no "passengers": everyone acts with initiative.

Trusting staff to act effectively and to make timely decisions appropriate to their level of responsibility also keeps people motivated to succeed. A workforce in which initiative is encouraged is more likely to stay with you.

the skills of leadership

Credibility as a leader

The characteristics we admire in our leaders, whether political, military, or business, do not change much. Essentially, leaders are rated on a series of traits that, taken together, contribute to the leader's ability to lead.

1 INTEGRITY

This might also be termed honesty. We want to trust our leaders, and when they are found to have lied, they lose face—and sometimes office, too. This term also encompasses moral judgment: We want to perceive our leaders as "playing fair" and dislike any sign of corruption. If a leader acts with integrity, it reflects on everyone he leads.

2 COMPETENCE

To be credible, a leader has to appear to be able to do the job. This might be a measure of experience—that is, we trust in competence because a leader has fulfilled a similar role already. It is not necessary to be the most technically gifted, for example. People skills are also part of a leader's competence.

3 INSPIRATION

We want leaders who make us feel good. A leader who can inspire others to act, especially in tough times or tricky situations, tends to earn and keep our respect and confidence. A leader who cannot inspire action in others is unlikely to be successful in either the short- or long-term.

4 PURPOSE AND DIRECTION

The more difficult the climate, the more we require our leaders to have a clear vision of the future and where the organization is headed. Leaders who can get their mission across and can deliver on what they say they will do are more likely to stay leaders.

5 CHARISMA

There is often an unquantifiable "extra" that makes the difference to a leader's credibility and defines the most successful. This might be summed up as charisma (see pp. 82–83).

Credibility as a leader continued

WHY CREDIBILITY MATTERS

Researchers have consistently shown that workers who believe they have a credible leader:

1 Are more highly motivated to succeed.

2 Believe their goals are more closely aligned with those of the organization.

3 Are eager to talk about where they work and the spirit in which they work.

4 Show a high degree of personal loyalty to the leader.

5 Have a greater sense of team spirit.

6 Feel supported and appreciated.

7 "Buy-in" for the long haul.

Leadership credibility, however, is about more than employees. It has a major part to play in attracting investors and customers and it also affects the organization's industry profile.

Fostering a sense of community

Common to many organizations or companies is a mission statement, a document that reflects the goals and standards of the organization. Employees know that, whatever their contribution, they are expected to reflec or exceed the mission statement.

WHAT'S IN A MISSION STATEMENT?

A statement might include such factors as:

1 Commitment to excellence in product quality

2 Commitment to people (both staff and customers)

3 Organizational pride

4 Measures of organizational success

TO FOSTER A SENSE OF COMMUNITY, LEADERS USE:

1 Shared purpose

2 Confidence

3 Affirmation

A successful leader fosters a sense of community by using his energy and dynamism to focus the beliefs of a constituent community to speak of reaffirming their core values.

The leader must use his genuine passion for the organization's goals to motivate all individuals to bring out the best by achieving a sense of common purpose.

This style of leadership requires great confidence both in self and in the message and its validity. Those being led are looking for a strong, positive, confident individual who will use drama to give the final resonance to the commitments that are being made.

the skills of leadership
Briefing

Briefing is the transfer of information from one individual to another, or one individual to a team of others, in order to reach a goal or target. The clarity with which the message is sent and understood defines the quality of a leader's ability to brief.

BRIEFING:

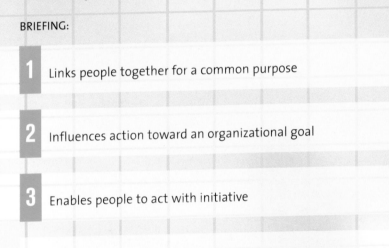

1 Links people together for a common purpose

2 Influences action toward an organizational goal

3 Enables people to act with initiative

A leader who cannot brief causes the organization to stagnate because activity and change cannot be effected.

BRIEFING STYLES:

1 Highly visible leaders may brief a whole team at a time. This ensures that all workers know that their contribution is acknowledged and valued and fosters the sense of community.

2 Alternatively, a leader may brief his senior managers or team leaders, whose task is then to disseminate the ultimate goal, while organizing their teams to reach it in the most effective and efficient manner.

3 A mix-and-match approach, briefing senior managers when information is sensitive but being visible to all when information can and needs to be shared.

Briefing continued

A SUCCESSFUL BRIEF:

1 Has a clearly defined goal or outcome.

2 Has a fixed time frame.

3 Is understood by all who are involved.

4 Ensures each individual involved knows his or her expected contribution.

5 Has a process for monitoring.

6 Has a time frame for monitoring, with key dates outlined.

7 Invites observation and feedback.

8 Incorporates flexibility, as long as the above criteria are met.

See also: Chapter 5, Motivation & Communication.

Organizing

The ability to get the necessary work done in the available time is attributable to a leader's ability to organize. This involves several key skill areas.

WHAT NEEDS TO BE DONE

The first stage in organizing anything is to define the task, for example:

1 Increase turnover by 20 percent

2 Improve quality

3 Develop a new management accounts system

4 Recruit a given number of volunteers or officers

5 Implement a training program for staff in a particular department

HOW WILL THE WORK BE DONE?

Most tasks can be split up into smaller constituent parts. A year-long project, for example, may involve four quarterly components, or a six-month research and a six-month development phase. Alternatively, different phases may overlap. For example, ground may be broken on a new building before the schedule of accommodation has been finalized.

A leader's role is to clarify the elements of the task and the order in which they should be achieved for optimum success.

WHEN WILL THE WORK BE DONE?

Few projects are open-ended. A leader's role is to fix a time frame, with key deadlines for individual tasks to be completed as well as to monitor and evaluate dates.

If a key deadline slips, it is also the leader's task (with his team members) to evaluate how and why, to get the project back on track, and to introduce more frequent dates for monitoring and evaluation.

WHO WILL DO THE WORK?

This may involve using existing teams, bringing in new people to strengthen existing teams, or amalgamating two or more teams if the task involves a synergistic approach.

A leader may also need to decide if any of his senior managers is more able than the current team leader to do the task and take appropriate action to ensure the best possible team is appointed to the task.

MARSHALING RESOURCES

Any task has financial and human costs. The leader's role is to evaluate the financial cost and either allocate resources from existing budgets or look at ways to raise the necessary funds. In addition, human costs (in terms of staff to cover staff allocated to the new project, or staff who have to be brought in specially) have to be added and evaluated.

MOTIVATION

Finally, to organize a team to complete a task on time and on budget, the leader has to motivate every individual involved to excel. See also Team Building, pp. 150–155 and Motivating, pp. 34–35.

HECKLIST: WHAT DOES ORGANIZING INVOLVE?

1 Evaluating what needs to be done in order to reach the desired outcome

2 Determining a methodology for undertaking the work

3 Fixing a time frame

4 Nominating individuals or groups to do the work

5 Freeing up financial and human resources to do the work

6 Encouraging individuals to do the task well

Motivating

Leaders must have the ability to motivate every single member of their workforce. A leaders who is visibly highly motivated himself is more likely to motivate others. Motivation ensures that the whole team maintains momentum and moves toward the organization's goal. Each team member may be motivated by different factors, but these have to be brought together by a leader for the good of the whole team. A leader needs to recognize that what motivated an individual even a few months ago, may not be an over-riding motivator now. He also needs to help individuals excel, for themselves and for the good of the team.

THE MAJOR MOTIVATORS

As an individual's career develops and progresses, his motivations may gradually change. At a given point, a worker is likely to be motivated by one or more of the following factors:

1 ACHIEVEMENT

The view that most individuals want a "quiet life" and are content to do the job and pick up the paycheck is outmoded. Research shows that people want to make a contribution. Leaders who offer encouragement for individuals to achieve the highest level possible are usually those who reap rich rewards.

2

RECOGNITION

People want their efforts and achievements to be recognized. Positive feedback and congratulations on a job well done are likely to encourage individuals to want to achieve more.

3

FINANCIAL REMUNERATION

Although money is a powerful motivator for many people, above a certain "comfort zone," it is less important than many managers once believed. Incentive schemes, productivity bonuses, and the like do not always yield the expected results. Conversely, if money is a major motivator, why do so many individuals place such high priority on their voluntary activities?

4

JOB SATISFACTION

Practicing or perfecting a skill, and using their intelligence in the workplace, leads to a greater interest in doing the job well. Working with like-minded colleagues for a common end also contributes greatly to job satisfaction.

the skills of leadership

Emotional intelligence

Your emotional intelligence (EQ) is your ability to understand and act on your own emotions and those of others. Most successful leaders have a high EQ.

Research has demonstrated that the most successful people in business, and in life itself, are not necessarily the most intellectually gifted.

Emotional intelligence is the ability to perceive, assess, and influence your own emotions and those of others, and it seems to have a greater influence on success than IQ.

Although a certain baseline level of knowledge is required in most managerial positions, these factors also influence effectiveness:

■ Sensitivity (or empathy, the ability to respond to how those around you are feeling)

■ Initiative (finding ways around frustrations and difficulties)

■ Communication (telling others how you feel)

■ Interpersonal skills (the ability to get along with others)

High EQ influences both individual performance and organizational productivity.

EN TIPS FOR ENHANCING YOUR EQ

1 Voice your feelings.

2 Take your emotions into account when decision making.

3 Surround yourself with people who make you feel good.

4 Understand that there is a difference between how you think and how you feel.

5 Know when and how to express emotions.

6 Be responsible for your own feelings.

7 Respect the feelings of other people.

8 Don't get mad: Channel anger into action.

9 Listen to what others have to say.

10 Understand underlying messages and lessons.

the skills of leadership

Controlling

When a plan has been agreed and the team has been briefed, the leader's next task is to control the team and the process.

"Control" has negative connotations, but a leader's control is not about controlling people but rather about effectively directing their activities. To achieve this centers around controlling projects, resources, and activities. It is constantly monitoring conditions and making adjustments in order to reach the desired objective.

TO MAINTAIN CONTROL, A LEADER NEEDS TO:

1 Plan, with goals, targets, standards, and objectives.

2 Collect feedback on what is happening.

3 Compare how things are with how they should be, if the goal is to be reached.

4 Recognize where improvement is needed.

5 Act to make those improvements.

In principle, a leader can monitor whether a plan is being implemented effectively by monitoring the people doing the work. In practice, this is impossible. The most successful way for a leader to exert control over a plan or project is to control its critical points. These are the factors that show up most clearly whether the plan is working. They could be:

■ Key dates attained

■ Manufacturing targets met

Striking a balance between maintaining the direction and interfering in the work of the group is critical. It is all too easy to move into a control mode giving no room for the development of individuals or new ideas.

The most effective control is when the team believes it has controlled itself. This is achieved by giving the team an understanding of the values and goals that will achieve success. Control is not simply monitoring, it is also maintaining direction to reach the goal.

Experimenting and risk taking

There can be no innovation without experimentation, which almost always involves an element of risk. A leader has to judge when that risk is acceptable.

GAMBLER OR RISK AVERSE?

■ Most people fall somewhere between these two extremes in most situations.

■ Some people gamble more than others.

■ Some people are gamblers when the stakes are not too high but are essentially conservative, or risk averse, when they are.

Because the consequences of failure can be high, most people do not gamble with their business decisions. However, in many fields it is precisely those who have gambled who reap the highest rewards.

Examples include industries such as share dealing, banking, and manufacturing. Stories abound of people of vision being unable to raise capital to put their ideas into action until one bank manager or lone investor gambled on them.

ASSESSING ACCEPTABLE RISK

Acceptable risk varies from company to company and project to project. Most leaders who are essentially risk averse would not thrive in a high-tech organization where product innovation was paramount, or in the futures market, for example. These industries, correctly, attract the gamblers. In any organization, however, you have to:

■ Understand the risks of a course of action (including doing nothing)

■ Make and implement your decisions accordingly

■ Accept that failure is always an option

KNOWING WHEN ENOUGH IS ENOUGH

You must have in place good and timely monitoring and feedback systems so that any risky project can be terminated before it puts the division, or even the organization itself, in jeopardy.

Evaluating

Whether a project is deemed a success or failure, it should be evaluated objectively, and its lessons should be learned and disseminated.

At key dates or stages during a project, a leader should get the whole team together to evaluate progress and share feedback. Center the session around such questions as:

1 What is going well?

2 Are we doing what we said we would do?

3 Where are we underachieving?

4 What is working and what isn't working?

5 How and where can we do better?

6 What lessons can we take from this project?

7 Would it make any difference if we were not engaged on this project?

8 How can we use what we have learned in a wider context (such as across different parts of the organization or on different teams)?

EFFECTIVE EVALUATION RELIES ON:

1 Having a project with clear and measurable goals and objectives.

4 Analyzing and interpreting the data.

2 Defining criteria for success or failure.

5 Using the evaluation to further the goals of the organization.

3 Collecting relevant data.

Envisioning the future

No one follows a leader who has no idea where he is headed: Another key to a leader's credibility is his forward thinking.

A leader's vision is to make a difference, and achieving his vision does make a difference. An exciting vision of the future:

1 Attracts investors.

2 Attracts workers.

2 Fosters a sense of community (see pp. 24–25).

HAVE A VISION

A leader's vision may be large or small, but what most people who have made a difference in the world (political, business, humanitarian, or environmental) say is that their vision started with a sense that things could be different, the past and present are not satisfactory, the future could be better. With that in mind, they set out to fine-tune the vision. This tends to happen in incremental stages.

1 KNOW YOUR PASSION

This can be a cause (such as homelessness), an institution (your alma mater), or the community (the local cub scouts). For many successful business leaders of the last decade or so, this has been new technology.

2 USE EXPERIENCE

Leaders are the sums of their past, good or bad. The past not only gives a time reference to a project, but more importantly, it shapes a vision. A previous success or failure in a given field enables a leader to focus on what might happen next.

Envisioning the future continued

3 KEEP YOUR EYES OPEN
Paying attention to what is happening now helps to shape future possibilities. Look at what is happening, and look at trends and patterns. However, spotting trends or being aware of what is happening does not pay dividends if a leader does not have a vision in the first place.

4 BE A LISTENER
Hear what others are saying, not only in your industry but also in politics and academia. These areas may be where the next big idea has its roots. Listening to people from different backgrounds, with different agendas, can help you to sharpen your vision.

5 BE A LEARNER
A vision of the future is in part a "feeling" about what is going to happen. This evolves from conducting research, selecting relevant information, and integrating experience with the current situation. Leaders are lifelong learners, never content to rest on past achievements.

FOCUS ON THE VISION

There are numerous barriers to vision, many of which are products of our own making. Chief among them might be termed "information overload." At any given time, so many pieces of information might be demanding attention that focusing on a vision becomes difficult. A leader focuses on two or three things that are most important and gets his team to do the same.

UNDERSTAND TWO CORE PRINCIPLES

1 A leader with a clear vision prompts people to move faster.

2 A leader with a vision gains people's trust.

Challenging the status quo

Few leaders who have made an impact take over an existing situation and run it as they happen to find it. At the heart of effective leadership is a wish to question the status quo.

Leaders are expected to effect change. Whether the leader is the CEO of a company or the president of a country, he has been placed in a position of authority by people who are unhappy with the way things are. His role is to make a difference.

Leaders are chosen for their ideas, creativity, and imagination. They are expected to take existing problems, shed new light upon them, and find a way forward. Whatever their style, they find a way to take people with them.

THE STATUS QUO IS OFTEN:

1 Faulty.

2 Based upon fear rather than rational thought.

3 Comfortable.

HANGE MIGHT BE PERCEIVED AS:

1 Worrying.

2 Harmful.

3 Invigorating.

A successful leader challenges the comfort, allays the fears, and fosters the feeling of invigoration by generating an understanding of the changes he is making.

Challenging the status quo is not usually about swift, massive change. Generally, successful leaders move in small steps.

KEYS TO MOUNTING AN EFFECTIVE CHALLENGE:
- A lot of small steps make a big difference.

- Change may bring success or failure.

- Change is invigorating.

Acknowledging contributions

In bad times, the leader may be the "fall guy," but good leaders know and acknowledge that they did not act alone.

Collaboration is increasingly the key to success. Pitting one team against another does not lead to enhanced performance: It is divisive and ultimately damaging.

As leaders are being asked to do more for less (treat more patients, enroll more students, produce more automobiles, satisfy more customers) on the same budget, for example, they realize that wiping away the competition is not the answer.

■ It is essential to be aware of and show that you have noted the efforts and contributions that all individuals have made toward a success.

■ In the future, this will allow you to coach individuals by drawing on good times and good performance when it may be necessary to motivate those you lead to improve and achieve more with less.

here is a need to celebrate the success of a team or a team member.

LEADER'S ROLE IS TO:

1 Set the agenda.

2 Give a framework for activity.

3 Monitor to ensure success.

4 Publicize the achievement.

The effect should be cumulative; it should build on success by identifying the success of others and using that to create an atmosphere of achievement. This is highly motivational.

the skills of leadership
Checklist

1 Nurture and develop the abilities of each and every team member.

2 Coach—whether in group or in individual situations.

3 Seize the moment: Sometimes it is necessary to challenge a team member, but mostly it pays to wait.

4 Accept errors: Individual errors are not important. You need to acknowledge errors but focus on each individual's strengths.

5 Prioritize: Tackling one or more weaknesses at a time is not likely to be successful.

6 Encourage emerging strengths.

7 List expectations: Every team member needs to know what you expect and when you expect delivery.

8 Encourage individuality: Do not expect people to do things your way, unless there is a very good reason why they should.

9 Identify other potential coaches in your team and nurture their talents.

2

what type of leader are you?

The commander

The most primitive leadership style is best summed up by the phrase "do it because I say so." Leaders who can only lead by command are limited in their success. Use this style with caution and only in limited situations.

HISTORICAL PERSPECTIVE

A legacy of corporate thinking from the last two centuries, command and control hierarchy is very common in large corporations across the world. There are many similarities to a military leadership, where orders and commands are issued and the expectation is of unthinking obedience.

The style, also known as coercive, has a rich and varied history: in fact, leaders operating in this way are often compared to Genghis Khan, a ruthless and feared leader of Mogul horsemen who conquered large areas of Asia and Europe during the medieval period. The style was successful then but is really not applicable today.

ESSENTIAL ELEMENTS

The style involves issuing orders or dictates without explanation or reason and maintaining tight central control of all decision making, reducing delegation, and imposing solutions on subordinate staff.

Although this chapter looks at leadership styles, the best leaders are chameleons, able to adapt their style to suit the situation. A successful leader may draw on elements of all the styles discussed in this chapter.

SHORTCOMINGS

Among the shortcomings of the command style are:

1 Failing to praise success and to motivate, which will lead to lowered morale.

2 Failing to provide one of the most effective leadership tools— a sense of common purpose.

3 Stifling initiative, which encourages subordinate managers with new ideas to leave the organization quickly.

4 Fostering little or no growth among potential leaders, as an atmosphere of fear and back-covering develops.

The commander continued

YOU NEED TO ADOPT THIS STYLE WHEN:

The command style is common, although of limited effectiveness. It is most effective and necessary:

1 In times of crisis (see pp. 74–77), when a strong centralized command is necessary

2 To break down existing failed practice in an organization where it is important to create new ways of thinking and working fast

It is unlikely to be effective in the long-term.

THE ELEMENTS REQUIRED TO BE A COMMAND STYLE OF LEADER ARE:

1 Emotional intelligence

2 Influence

3 Achievement

4 Perhaps most importantly, the ability to seize the opportunity

If you can issue an order on the spot, can make a swift decision without hesitation because you understand the goals to be achieved, and have the emotional intelligence to pick an appropriate course of action and communicate this without ambiguity, you have the hallmarks of a command style leader.

Team leader

Those who apply the team leader style of leadership tend to know and understand the people in an organization more than the structures and goals. Also known as the affiliate style of leadership, it focuses on the emotional needs of employees.

THE TEAM LEADER STRIVES TO ACHIEVE AN EMOTIONAL EMPATHY BY:

1 Fostering harmony within the organization.

2 Promoting friendly relations and interactions.

3 Fostering a nurturing environment that values the contribution of all individuals.

A team leader fosters emotional empathy in the quieter times in any business cycle. This is very valuable because she can then use this cohesiveness when the pressure is on to perform.

ADVANTAGES OF THE STYLE

1 Acting in this way will boost morale and may well help employees and other team members to work effectively and efficiently through the more mundane and routine tasks or time because of the shared sense of achievement that you, as team leader, have created.

2 Organizations in which this style of leadership is practiced are flexible and resilient because the team spirit and trust engendered will allow for swift changes of work patterns to meet changing demands and to work through a crisis.

3 The spirit of cooperation that is created will also make an organization more likely to succeed in a rapidly changing marketplace.

Team leader continued

A classic example of the team leader style of management is in the field of sports: managers who have built up a rapport with the team they lead and motivate achieve far more through understanding team members' individual needs and aspirations. When the goal is to win, the team leader style is particularly successful.

SHORTCOMINGS OF THE STYLE

1 The downside of this style is the inevitable need to achieve.

2 Although organizations may be flexible, they may lack a clear goal orientation. Team members may feel rudderless.

3 The style tends to emphasize praise and rarely corrects poor performance. This can lead to mediocrity with a consequent reduction in productivity and efficiency.

4 Individuals may become indistinguishable from the rest of the team and lack drive and direction.

These potential negative outcomes mean that the style is best practiced along with an element of visionary or empowerment styles to ensure not only that operations are clearly defined but also that the benefits of this style are achieved.

RE YOU A GOOD TEAM LEADER?

1 Is there a high level of morale in your team?

2 Do your organization and team rise to new challenges and change the way they work to fit changing and challenging circumstances?

3 Is your organization successful in a rapidly changing business environment?

If you answer "yes" to these questions, you are already an effective team leader.

Empowerment or democratic

A democratic leadership style relies entirely on the strength of the individual leader to plan and delegate effectively.

An empowering leader ensures a clear purpose and goals, understands the strengths of individuals within the organization, and gives them the scope and authority to operate and fulfill their potential.

ELEMENTS OF THE STYLE
This is a leadership style that encompasses coaching skills to focus on personal development of individuals within the organization and needs the time to develop an understanding of their motivation. This requires the time to go beyond short-term issues and explore each individual employee's dreams and life goals in order to know how to motivate her.

The leader needs to ensure that those she leads understand the goals and objectives of the organization and to give them the knowledge they need to work for the common good.

Such leaders ensure that the individuals within the organization are aware of how their own goals and objectives can be aligned with those of the organization. This is achieved by focusing on positive emotional responses to a given situation because the leader has established trust and rapport. This fosters an environment in which employees are willing and able to listen to and respond positively to performance feedback.

The democrat must be prepared to listen to the team members and modify her position to accommodate the individuals' views on how a project can be successfully accomplished.

Empowerment or democratic continued

This style of leadership requires good delegation, with challenging assignments being given to individuals to help stretch and develop them in a supportive environment. Failure is accepted but treated as a learning experience, leading to better future performance.

A good empowering leader is one who is able to demonstrate a belief in potential and is willing to take the time to invest in individuals' personal development. The result is motivated employees who strive to uphold the standards and work with greater autonomy at higher performance levels.

WHEN THE STYLE DOES NOT WORK

The style may fail when applied in an area were the employees lack motivation and so require an excessive amount of supervision and support that will undo the trust that has been developed. If the leader is too focused on outcomes and is too goal orientated, empowerment may become more like micromanagement of the situation with the team being given little room to operate on its own initiative.

AN YOU:

1 Recognize the need to sell the ideas to, and gain the allegiance of, team members?

2 Listen to the responses, views, and requirements of team members, and adhere to them?

3 Understand the motivations and aspirations of each and every team member?

4 Include elements of other leadership styles, in particular, the coaching style?

If you answer "yes" to these questions, you are a democratic leader, or can use this style effectively.

Goal oriented or pace setting

The need for goal setting and having a focus for the organization's operation is self-evident. The effects of failing to supply sufficient leadership of this type are usually characterized by failure to make profit or to prosper. An over-emphasis on the goal and too much pace setting can have negative effects on the organization, however.

THIS STYLE IS OFTEN SEEN AS THE MOST APPROPRIATE ONE TO USE:

1 Its attention to detail is admirable.

2 The style is typified by expectations of high standards of performance linked with a concern for doing things better and faster.

3 It can be good for fostering teamwork and collaboration, a sense that everyone is in it together and working for the common good.

Used sparingly, these can be seen as "good" traits. However, overuse of this style can leave employees feeling pushed too hard and— due to a lack of coaching and failure to give clear guidelines— unable to meet the high performance expected of them.

OVERUSE OF THIS LEADERSHIP STYLE RESULTS IN:

1 A decline in morale.

2 An increase in staff turnover (often of staff who are the best but who feel unappreciated because of the leader's focus on achievement and her failure to acknowledge their input).

3 An inability to see the "big picture" (by setting lots of small goals, the overall focus of where the organization is headed can be lost).

Goal oriented or pace setting continued

The consequence of a lack of trust between leader and team can be for a leader whose sole methods are pace setting to become ever more obsessed with the targets and achievement, inducing a kind of downward spiral as the members of the team become increasingly frustrated as they feel forced to achieve more with less.

The style will in itself begin to add to the problems of a failing organization. As additional unrealistic goals are set, the team will not be able to achieve them.

There are times when goal orientation is a necessary style to adopt, for example when seizing a new opportunity or pushing through a change, but the long-term effects of using only the style may well be negative. Concentration on the task and goals can lead to a failure to listen to individuals in the team and to recognize the need for an effective feedback and communication system.

This can result in alienation and the leader's message becoming counterproductive. As is often the case, the style of goal orientation is most effective when it is used in conjunction with other techniques.

Goal orientation, if used sparingly and with other effective styles, has the effect of raising the standards of performance of the whole team.

Leaders who are pace setters tend to be interested in learning new approaches to achieve their goals and in seizing opportunity.

This style may work best in collaborating with the coaching or team leader styles (see pp. 60–63).

Because the coach leads by "showing how" something should be done, the individuals and the organization can be successful.

The pace setter as leader can be viewed as the norm in situations where high performance is expected, for example, in the financial industry where individual performance is easily measured. Often, in situations where the goals are not so clear-cut, a pacesetter will have to define the "winning post," to show how success can be achieved and measured.

Leadership by example or visionary

Of all leadership styles, leadership by example is the one in which the leader believes in the goals to be achieved and in the methods employed. This style calls for a high degree of awareness of the setting of the operations of the organization and of the targets to be achieved. The style is inspirational, best summed up by "do as I do" not the "do as I say" of the command and control leader nor the "do it or else" of the goal-orientated leader.

A leader by example is a visionary who is committed to removing internal barriers within organizations to improve communication and foster a common purpose for all employees or team members. Honesty is an underlying tenet of such a style, because there is an emotional commitment to the beliefs that are shown as examples to be followed. For example, the style tends toward inclusiveness by improving communication and distributing information to foster organizational success.

The visionary leader is also one who espouses "management by walking around," that is, needing to understand the problems of the organization firsthand and then being able to inspire improvement and change through active use of this detailed knowledge.

For this style to work, you have to have a sense of the emotional responses of your employees and to understand their motivations. There are elements of this style in both the empowering and coaching leadership styles.

WHEN IT IS NOT APPROPRIATE

Although generally an effective style—particularly when used to turn around failing or languishing organizations—there are circumstances when its use may not be appropriate. In these circumstances, a more direct authoritarian approach will reduce confusion and give a clear, unambiguous course of action with a short time frame.

The style should be used with caution in an academic setting. When there is a team of experts or peers of the leader, it is essential to ensure that a vision is in step with the majority. Often individuals need to avoid appearing pompous, arrogant, or negative toward their team members. That said, the use of leadership by example, in many instances, results in good short- and long-term outcomes.

Crisis leadership

There are extreme and unusual situations that call for a different and unique
of leadership to overcome the immediate problems: These situations are not
about maintainance—they are about survival.

Examples of this type of situation range from the need to fight off a hostile takeover bid to the challenge of leading in wartime or in a terrorist situation. The most high-profile examples of crisis leadership in modern times are perhaps Winston Churchill's leadership as prime minister of the United Kingdom during World War II and Rudolph Giuliani's time as mayor in the aftermath of the September 11 terrorist attack on New York City.

THE STYLES THESE TWO LEADERS HAD IN COMMON ARE:

1 An understanding of the needs of the people who were being led

2 A belief in the truth and values that the individuals concerned stood for

3 A knowledge of how and what to communicate to those being led

4 An empathy with the populations and an understanding of the values and concerns of those individuals

In a crisis, the command and control style springs straight to the top of the list. However, this is applied by the best leaders with a number of other styles; they understand what motivates the people being led, employing the visionary and team builder styles as well. There is no doubt that both Churchill and Giuliani succeeded in crisis situations because they understood the motivators for the populations they were leading, but also because they could communicate the vision of how things should and could be and used the best talents available from the people around them.

There is also a need to keep emotional control, which enables them to reach beyond the immediate crisis and allow those being led to focus on achievements.

what type of leader are you?

Decision making in an emergency

In an emergency, the skills of leadership do not change, but it becomes more important to act quickly and incisively.

1 Assess the situation.

2 Gather around you the people who can give you the information you need.

3 Set up an appropriate communications system.

4 Make a plan.

5 Make decisions.

6 Communicate clearly and unambiguously.

7 Set short deadlines.

8 Identify key individuals.

9 Look for reports from key individuals.

10 Establish a reporting time frame and stick to it rigidly.

11 Acknowledge and praise contributions.

12 Keep communication lines open.

KEY QUESTIONS

3

self-analysis

self-analysis

Professional knowledge

The technical, or professional, knowledge you need to lead effectively depends on your business and the part of the organization in which you operate.

PROFESSIONAL KNOWLEDGE CAN BE CONSIDERED IN TWO WAYS:

1 Strategic knowledge: this is an understanding of your business, industry, and company. It is this knowledge that enables you to predict trends and motivate your managers.

2 Technical knowledge: this is the ability to manufacture a component, use a piece of software, or design a new product.

Junior managers need technical knowledge. They must know how to produce goods, give logical answers, and so on. They do not necessarily need to see "the big picture."

Middle managers need strategic and technical knowledge. They need sufficient technical knowledge to manage production and appraise staff, but they also must have the strategic vision to motivate their juniors.

Senior managers must be technically proficient, but they need to have strategic vision to run the company and to set and achieve goals. They must see the "big picture."

SETTING THE RIGHT BALANCE

■ If you rely on your own technical knowledge, rather than on your managers to manage the technical side, you should work on improving your strategic vision.

■ On the other hand, if your lack of technical knowledge means that you misrepresent to clients and customers what your team can achieve, you need to gain more technical knowledge.

■ It is generally a given that managers have an adequate technical knowledge. However, if you work in an industry where change is rapid, you may start to lack the technical knowledge you need to manage effectively.

■ Ways to keep your technical know-how up to speed include: networking, reading the trade press, attending conferences, using your trade or professional association, and writing and delivering trade talks and speeches.

self-analysis

Do you have charisma?

Charisma is not tangible. It does not really depend on looks, manner, or personality, but all these factors can contribute toward it.

ASK YOURSELF THESE QUESTIONS:

1 Do people listen to you?

2 Do people act on what you say?

3 Do reports of what you have said get passed on to others?

4 Do people follow your lead?

If you can answer "yes" to all of the above, you have a good measure of charisma already and can build on it.

O BUILD CHARISMA:

1 Analyze what motivates your audience.

2 Interpret what makes them happy.

3 Tailor your message to the group you are addressing.

4 Work out what works for your constituents. Give them more of the same.

HE UNDERLYING MESSAGE

- Identify with your audience.
- Establish major motivators.
- Give them what they want to hear.

Grasping the situation

A leader has to be able to appreciate when a situation is serious and act accordingly. A leader who does not have the ability to understand the various elements of a problem and decide what to do about them has failed.

Your reading of a situation and the actions you subsequently take in response demonstrate your understanding of your organization's aims and limitations. To show he has understood his organization's direction, the leader should:

1 CALL IN ALL RELEVANT DATA

Use all departments and outside sources to piece together the facts and determine what is speculation.

2 SEPARATE OUT DIFFERENT TYPES OF INFORMATION

Quickly pull out relevant data and information, as opposed to irrelevant background noise. Separating data from any given situation and converting it into usable information requires rapid analytical skills and a coherent approach to organizing facts.

3 KEEP NOTES OF MAJOR POINTS
A good trick is to use different colored highlighters or different pages
of a flip chart for different types of information to make it easier to
access the major facts quickly and accurately.

4 DEVELOP A HIERARCHICAL APPROACH
In some companies and situations, different parts of the "problem"
(such as financial or environmental) will be more important than
others. Rank each area separately, and deal with the most important
issues first.

5 COMMUNICATE
Make communication swift, and set in place a system for updating it.

self-analysis
Decision-making ability

Confidence in their own decision-making ability sets successful leaders apart from the rest of the pack.

A decision does not necessarily need to be the best decision; however, it does need to be positive, especially when there is an element of uncertainty or doubt as to the best course of action to follow.

■ How often do you think you have made the right decision?
■ How often do you think you have made the wrong decision and lived with the consequences?
■ Do you find it difficult to make decisions at all?

A NUMBER OF METHODS ASSIST EFFECTIVE DECISION MAKING. MIX AND MATCH FROM THESE APPROACHES TO SEE WHAT WORKS FOR YOU:

1

RISK ANALYSIS
This is a systematic approach to analyzing various factors, mainly known but some unknown. An effective leader uses specialists to advise on analyzing risk.

2 DECISION TREES
A decision tree lists, like branches of a tree, key factors that influence a decision, as well as possible outcomes and potential chance events. By looking at all the relevant details of alternative courses of action, a leader can reach a decision.

3 PREFERENCE THEORY
Preference or utility theory applies a statistical probability to the success or failure of a decision. This is normally expressed in terms of a percentage of success. Leaders are often risk averse and will take the course with the highest percentage of success. Some leaders will take a course of action with a higher risk when the rewards from the action are overwhelmingly greater than the safe course of action.

4 OPTION APPRAISAL
Considering alternative options from both financial and qualitative requirements may be used as a method for arriving at a well thought-out, logical decision.

self-analysis
Creativity

Creativity is the ability to offer new ways of doing things and an innovative approach to problem solving.

HOW ABLE ARE YOU TO:

1 Come up with new ideas?

2 Be original?

3 Deliver intuitive solutions to problems?

These are the areas where a leader is able to make a difference. To generate creativity in yourself and others, be aware of your own strengths and weaknesses and use them.

1 Don't be afraid to ask questions: Most people with specialist knowledge will share advice with fellow professionals.

2 Look at how other people do things, especially in successful organizations, to try to identify what makes them successful; then adapt and apply their practices to your way of working.

3 Take the ideas, information, and skills of your team members, and use them.

4 Aim to learn one new thing every day.

5 Be open and receptive to the input of others.

6 Constantly seek out new ways of looking at each task that's set.

Job satisfaction

Your own job satisfaction will be a factor in how you perform and how you lead. The exercise of leadership power may be the satisfaction in itself, but it is more likely that the effect your actions have on others and on particular situations will generate the satisfaction.

THE FACTORS THAT AFFECT JOB SATISFACTION ARE:

1 The extent to which your sphere of operation is limited.

2 The level of financial control you have.

3 Your authority to hire and fire individuals who work for you.

4 Selection of your own team members.

5 The amount of time that you have to produce creditable reports or feedback.

6 The remuneration package (although this is often less a factor than managers, and their subordinates, believe).

The number of intervening layers between yourself and the chief executive will also affect the level of satisfaction; the more layers, the less satisfaction you are likely to have.

This may be because your scope of control of your activity will be limited and your ability to motivate and develop new ideas will also be controlled.

However, if the reporting structure is convoluted, you may be able to operate in an independent manner without the need for upward reference.

Autonomy can contribute greatly to job satisfaction, although it may increase the level of risk taking by team members (which might start to become unacceptable).

Mental flexibility

Mental flexibility is essentially the ability to juggle different activities simultaneously and to be able to respond effectively to new, complex, or problematic situations.

Successful leaders develop ways of coping with different activities without being overwhelmed or diverted by irrelevancies.

The essential skill is to handle conflicting data and to see through to the information underlying any conflicts, being able to sort out the relevant facts and to disregard and reject inappropriate information that only clouds the issue.

LEADERS HAVE TO:

1 Agree to priorities in advance.

2 See in all situations how those priorities can be met.

3 See things from several different perspectives.

4 Articulate the priorities into your vision of how things are to be and the actions required achieving them.

 5 Take risks.

6 Switch from practical to nonpractical thinking.

 7 Accept ambiguity or uncertainty.

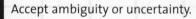

THE EFFECT OF TIME

Time pressure is often an issue. The need for mental flexibility does not mean that, while you are weighing options, things can be allowed to drift. An effective leader needs to think fast, making the correct decision in a timely manner, rather than spending too much time ponderously considering all the alternative scenarios.

Applying a clear vision of the priorities to a given situation enables a leader to retain mental flexibility without losing sight of the essential, focused drive to achieve the proper outcome.

self-analysis

Proactivity

The leader in any organization will need to be proactive. Without this skill, your organization is likely to drift and lack direction.

THIS IS HOW TO BE PROACTIVE:

1 TAKE THE INITIATIVE
The successful leader will always be looking to take the initiative; he does not wish to allow circumstances to dictate his course of action.

2 GET THINGS DONE
Making things happen is the credo for the leader. A leader should take every opportunity to develop new ways of thinking and acting, taking the best from any ideas presented and turning them into action.

3 CHALLENGE YOURSELF AND OTHERS
The successful leader looks for new ideas and skills from outside his current sphere of activity, to prepare new ways of doing things; he is willing and able to challenge others with these ideas.

4 TAKE CHARGE

Generally, the leader presses to ensure that things don't simply happen to him but that he makes things happen, by planning and implementing, by guiding and controlling the actions of the others in his team.

You cannot be at the mercy of events; you must be in charge of them.

It is essential to be the motivator and it is better to be leading from in front than pushing from behind. Constantly be on the lookout for ways to enhance creativity, using techniques such as brainstorming and groups such as "think tanks" to overcome creeping inertia.

self-analysis

Moral courage

Moral courage is the ability to do what is proper, rather that what is popular or convenient, without regard for personal reputation.

Physical courage is easy to understand: It makes ordinary people perform extreme acts without regard for physical safety. Moral courage, by contrast, is more difficult to pinpoint. It is easier to describe people who act with moral courage than to define precisely what it is.

Acting with moral courage is making decisions based on fairness, empathy, and respect for others. It is also acting with honesty and with a sense of responsibility. It is decision making that does not take into account personal gain, self-esteem, or reputation.

MORAL COURAGE INVOLVES:

1 Drawing a distinction between right and wrong.

2 Recognizing when something is wrong or unfair, and doing something about it.

3 Defending those who are unable to defend themselves.

 4 Upholding justice.

 5 Setting an example that inspires others to act well.

 5 Taking a stand over something you believe to be right.

The negative effects of acting with moral courage may be:

▪ Financial loss

▪ Lack of career advancement

▪ Damaged relationships

Acting with moral courage involves taking a risk, pitting yourself against a problem that others cannot handle, laying yourself on the line. The bonus, however, is the knowledge that you have done the right thing in trying circumstances.

self-analysis

Psychological resilience

Resilience is an individual's ability to thrive in spite, or perhaps because, of life's stress

LEADERS WITH PSYCHOLOGICAL RESILIENCE TEND TO:

 1 See problems as opportunities.

 2 Make the most of every opportunity, no matter how fleeting.

 3 Be unfazed by setbacks that restrict others.

 4 Ride out bad times, in the belief that good ones are on the way.

 5 Handle situations of a difficult or complex nature.

 6 Learn from hardships.

7 Have a good support network.

Resilience is not a skill that leaders are born with. It can be learned and developed by anyone who practices it.

STEPS TO DEVELOPING RESILIENCE:

■ Make connections: A supportive network of family and friends builds resilience.

■ Treat crises as surmountable: Accept that bad things are going to happen, but modify your approach to them.

■ Treat life as a voyage of self-discovery: Constantly find ways to build on your skills and find ways to take positives from negative life events.

■ Accept change: Focus on what you can do, not what you can't.

■ Be goal-centered: Take small steps to reach your goal.

■ Act decisively: Don't wait for something to happen.

■ Think positively: Have confidence in your own abilities.

■ Remain optimistic: Focus on what you want.

self-analysis

Pragmatism

An effective leader must be pragmatic: knowing what is possible, what is useful, what can be changed, and what is impossible given any given current constraints of the situation.

Pragmatism forwards the objectives of the organization. The central theme of a pragmatist's view of the world is a belief in the utility of all functions. Pragmatists judge all situations and courses of action against whether or not the action will improve a given situation.

It can be seen as a way of considering all the alternatives at the start of a project to establish clearly in your mind the areas where success can be achieved and those areas where there is little chance of success. In this way, you emphasize the positive areas and avoid the negative ones.

A LEADER APPLIES HIS PRAGMATISM TO DETERMINE:

1 The worth of an idea.

2 How effective a course of action will be when it is put into operation.

3 What sort of return on the investment of time and activity will come from the idea.

4 The effort that individuals will need to put into an action.

5 The relative inputs of each member of the team to an operation of the organization.

6 Whether one member of the team is more effective and should be given the leading role.

7 Whether a financial investment will bring greater rewards than not investing (this may also be based on the perceived risk of implementing the idea, see pp. 40–41).

Restraint

Being able to act with restraint and being able to understand the limitation of your own authority are essential. It is important to know how to be firm and resilient without becoming dogmatic.

1 Avoid statements that are a harsh or negative: Attempt to use positive reinforcement rather than negative criticism.

2 Use anger sparingly and then only to emphasize the results that you want to achieve.

3 Keep control in all situations, particularly when you are tired or under stress; it may be particularly difficult to be restrained in such situations, but the qualities that you engender in your team will be a reflection of your own attitudes.

4 Take breaks: When situations or events shift your perspective, stand back. Hasty actions at the wrong time can cause long-term problems.

EPARATING BEHAVIOR AND PEOPLE

▓ In difficult situations, it is important to distinguish between the person and the behavior he is displaying and to try to see beyond the immediate situation.

▓ The patience you display in defusing potentially damaging situations will pay dividends in motivating the team.

▓ You need to communicate the worth you see in an individual and his overall contribution to the team, rather than the frustration you feel from the behavior that individual is currently exhibiting.

self-analysis
Micromanagement

Responsible for the downfall of many leaders, micromanagement is a failure of leadership. A leader who micromanages is not managing effectively.

Attention to detail is important, and that is undeniable. However, don't confuse attention to detail with micromanagement.

ATTENTION TO DETAIL IS:

1 Knowing what other people are doing.

2 Trusting them to do it.

3 Understanding the processes which your team members are using.

4 Seeing how the constituent parts of the big picture fit together.

MICROMANAGEMENT IS:

1 Not trusting others to act.

2 Constantly meddling in tasks that you have, correctly and justifiably, already delegated.

3 Doing yourself what is somebody else's responsibility.

4 A failure of supervision.

5 Taking your eyes off the big picture.

Social skills

Effective leaders use their social skills to get productivity from others within the team they lead; this in part derives from understanding the motivations c individuals in a team.

Social skills will enable you to get on with other people in a productive way. This will enable all members of the team to achieve to the best of their abilities and to make the team more effective than the sum of the efforts of individual team members.

USE YOUR SOCIAL SKILLS BY:

1 Being sympathetic to the needs of the team while keeping in mind the needs of the organization.

2 Being empathetic with the motives of all members of the team and with the goals of the organization.

3 Being supportive of team members with problems, understanding their current motivations and frustrations.

4 Handling conflict effectively to reduce the friction within a group and make the best working environment.

5 Assertively handling hostility whether from inside the team or from the organization.

6 Exploiting all social possibilities—to network, to find new staff or clients, to explore new business avenues and opportunities, to source new materials.

Self-knowledge

Constantly reassessing where you are and where you want to be, based on your beliefs and value systems, is the way to keep abreast of what is happening in the business world and your place within it.

1 REVIEWING YOUR BELIEFS
What do you believe in, and why?
Religion
Family
Country
Money
Education
Personal accountability

2 WHAT DON'T YOU LIKE?
What makes you mad, hurt, disappointed?
Waste (of talent, resources, life)
Inefficiency
Selfishness
Betrayal
Irresponsibility

3

WHAT ARE YOUR GREATEST JOYS?
What makes you smile, laugh, be thankful that you are here now?
Deal well struck
Family
Leisure / travel
Intellectual challenge

4

WHAT DO YOU FEAR?
What makes you lie awake at night, or paralyzes you during the day?
Threat of war or terrorism
Fears of your children's safety
Health worries (physical, mental)
Ecological problems
Losing your job
Relationship breakdown

5

REVIEWING YOUR BEHAVIOR
How does your value system affect the way you behave?
Personally (as partner, parent, child)
Socially (with friends, colleagues, other moms and dads)
Organizationally (with superiors and subordinates, with clients
and complainants, when negotiating, hiring, and firing)

KEY QUESTIONS

The ability to learn from experience

No one has seen it all and done it all. Many times you will be faced with an unfamiliar situation. How well you deal with it will depend on your ability to learn from what has gone before.

1

REFLECTING ON INCIDENTS AT WORK

This means having the analytical ability to clarify why something worked in one situation, and how that can be applied to different situations, perhaps in a different industry or working environment. Something from outside work could also give you cues as to how you should approach a business problem.

This also includes learning from your own mistakes and taking positives from essentially negative outcomes.

2

UNDERSTANDING YOUR OWN REACTIONS

Part of a continuous process in your current position is to know how events in this company or organization and the decisions you have made could be modified, if they were unsuccessful, or reapplied when they worked.

3 EXPLORING THE ACTIONS AND REACTIONS OF OTHERS
In any situation, knowing how others react and what those around you
are going to counsel is important. This does not mean that you should
not ask for their opinions, but you should be aware ahead of time how
others are going to act and what their reactions to your proposals are
likely to be. You should also be prepared to modify your ideas.

4 CONSIDERING HOW PEOPLE MIGHT BE HANDLED DIFFERENTLY IN
THE FUTURE
As you work with different professionals from different backgrounds,
with different skills, aspirations, and enthusiasms, you will build a
picture of who will do what successfully and who to trust to handle
different tasks and problems. Knowing which tasks to place with
which individuals comes with experience, and experience is gained by
analyzing your previous successes and failures.

self-analysis
Your leadership personality

Your leadership personality has a great impact on your interaction with the team. Consider these leadership styles and where you fit.

COMMANDING
This style has the advantage of certainty in uncertain times because it relieves team members of any decision making. It works well with "problem" employees and when a total shift in direction is the only way forward.
Effect on team: Generally negative

DEMOCRATIC
This style gets the most from employees and is ideal when you really need people on your side. It can be highly motivating but relies on consensus.
Effect on team: Usually highly positive

3

VISIONARY

Motivating team members toward a shared goal is an ideal style if change is needed within an organization.
Effect on team: Positive

4

TEAM LEADER

By allying individual talents with organizational goals, this style usually builds an effective team working to a common purpose.
Effect on team: Positive

5

PACE SETTING

This style relies on a competent and motivated team to start with but can be highly effective in meeting challenging goals. It relies on good management.
Effect on team: Positive when management is effective, but if management is weak, it can be highly negative

self-analysis

Your leadership personality continued

Consider these statements and the degree to which you agree with them. Then think about whether your team would agree or disagree with your ratings. Your working situation and your level of authority will influence some of these factors, but you should gain an insight into your leadership personality and how you could modify it, if necessary.

1 I think it is vital to plan the work of my team, and that includes effective planning of my own time.

2 I am naturally creative, and my ability to come up with different solutions often gets me and my team out of difficulties.

3 I like to involve my team in making decisions that affect the team.

4 I am sensitive to others' needs.

5 I am level-headed and even-tempered, whatever the situation.

6 I have a clear vision of the future. I have communicated this vision to my team, and they understand it.

7 My team knows that I want results, and that I will do everything I can to make timely decisions to get speedy results.

8 I am always enthusiastic and energetic about work.

 9 I am a good communicator, whatever the forum.

If you agree strongly with all of these statements, you have an excellent blend of leadership characteristics, enabling you to create a strong team and direct it effectively.

If you disagree strongly with these statements and are in a position of leadership, it is likely that your power rests on your technical or professional knowledge, or that you are relying on the power that goes with your position within the organization rather than your "pure" leadership ability.

self-analysis

Self-directed learning

Effective leadership involves self-directed learning, that is, the ability to see who you really are and who you really want to be and to work to create a situation in which the two are allied.

This process is not a continuum, or a timeline, and there is no real end point. All the factors along the way are interlinked; some will take longer to master than others. What happens is that as you practice, spending time and effort on new skills, they become part of your repertoire, part of the ideal you.

1 WHO DO YOU WANT TO BE?
- What are the skills and attributes I value?
- What will motivate me to be the person I value?
- What are the strengths I want to acquire?

2 WHO ARE YOU?
- What are my strengths?
- What are my weaknesses?
- How do I relate to others?
- Do I know how others see me?

3 HOW DO 1 AND 2 DIFFER?
- What is the skills' mismatch between the person I am and the person I want to be?
- What is the attributes' mismatch between the person I am and the person I want to be?
- What is the overall mismatch between the person I am and the person I want to be?

4 WHAT IS YOUR TIME FRAME FOR SUCCESS?
- How can I build on my strengths?
- How can I master my weaknesses?
- How long will it take to gain mastery of the skills and attributes I lack?
- How much will I need to practice?
- Is external help available?
- What is my action plan?

KEY QUESTIONS

Self-directed learning continued

5 HOW CAN YOU PRACTICE?
- Can I use new skills in my existing situation?
- Do I need more learning or training opportunities?
- Is there a supportive team to help me gain in competence and ability?
- Am I inviting feedback?
- How do I put into action what I am being told?

6 CAN YOU ACHIEVE CHANGE?
- Do I realize I have changed?
- Is my leadership style more effective?
- Do I have the support and trust of the team?

7 HOW CAN YOU MONITOR PERFORMANCE?
- Can I check the outcome of different strategies?
- Am I able to question the suitability of the skills I used?
- Can I analyze on an ongoing basis the gaps in my skills base?

8

CAN YOU REINFORCE SUCCESS?
- Am I learning from success and accepting new ideas?
- Can I apply different skills to different situations?

9

CAN YOU SUSTAIN IMPROVEMENT?
- Can I practice my new skills?
- Can I continue to improve and build on my skills?
- Can I continue to experiment with new ideas?

KEY QUESTIONS

4

situational analysis &
team building

situational analysis & team building

Knowing the organization

Understanding an organization, its culture, and its vocabulary is key to successfully leading it.

All organizations are different in the way they approach and solve problems, and delegate authority. As a leader within an organization, it is essential to understand the culture and nature of the organization, so that you are in tune with the perceived way of achieving success there.

The culture will influence both the way things are done and the measures of success or failure. It is essential to understand and use the appropriate language of an organization.

The operation of a multinational organization is very different from an organization based in one or two cities. The style and culture of a healthcare operation will not be the same as a media company, a publishing group, or a government body.

Different companies have different ways of seeing the market and the business environment in which they operate. This view influences the way the organization conducts its business, and the values it emphasizes.

You will need to know and be able distinguish several different factors of the organization you lead, although there are some common factors that influence the culture. For example:

1 Do senior managers address each other by their first names?

2 What is the dress code of the organization?

These may seem insignificant, but they give clues to the underlying deeply held views and expectations of the organization.

Understanding what is distinctive and the values of your organization will assist you in being a successful leader.

Knowing the organization continued

The expectations and goals of any organization are normally unique to that organization. What is the "emphasis" of the organization you lead?

1 Increased productivity

2 Product innovation or creativity

3 High public esteem

4 Decreased costs

5 Increased profits

6 Satisfied shareholders

7 Raised market share

8 Customer satisfaction

9 Low staff turnover

10 Client retention

11 Autonomy / control

12 Adherence to specified procedures and working methods

13 High-profile, hierarchical management

Knowing the organization continued

A motivated workforce will produce results for you. Ask which of these statements best sum up how your employees feel about the organization, then canvas their views.

- This is a great place to work.

- The organization now has some "get up and go."

- It's getting better, but there's still room for improvement.

- Conditions were better . . . (before the management buyout, under the former CEO, when we were in the old facility).

- The organization has gone downhill recently.

- I like and respect my colleagues.

- We work effectively.

- We work efficiently.

- The waste of time and money is appalling.

- Most of my colleagues are time servers.

- I no longer tell people where I work.

- I'm proud we still do things in the time-honored way.

- Initiative is encouraged.

- Initiative is stifled.

- There are too many managers and too few do-ers.

- Members of management are complacent.

- My colleagues are complacent.

- There is a creative "buzz" about the place now.

- I don't think anyone really has a plan.

- The organization's goals and objectives are clear, and I want to be part of them.

situational analysis & team building
Knowing the organization continued

The words and phrases that appear in your company literature can offer good clues as to how the people who work for you see themselves, and how your management team exercises authority.

1
COMPANY LITERATURE: THE POSITIVES
Celebrate
Clarity
Create
Dynamic
Effective
Incentives
Innovate
Initiative
Investors
Promotion
Recruitment
Team building
Training

2 REPORTS ABOUT THE COMPANY: THE NEGATIVES
Bureaucracy
Centralized
Closure
Confusion
Control
Downsizing
Exclusion
Meetings
Outplacement
Redundancy
Retrenchment
Suspension
Uncertainty

3 WORDS THAT COULD BE POSITIVE OR NEGATIVE
Cohesive
Focused
Rebranding
Restructuring
Strategic
Timely

Leadership as a continuum

The behavior leaders use is affected by the environment in which they are working. They will also have to adapt and change their techniques to suit the situation. There is a continuum along which the leader has more or less freedom to operate. In the box below, the points are on a scale.
The statements at the top show the leader's freedoms are unrestricted; the statements at the bottom show the opposite.

LEADER FREE TO ACT, TEAM RESTRICTED

■ Leader is able to make decisions, which team members accept.

■ Leader must "sell" decisions to get acceptance from team members.

■ Leader presents decisions and must respond to questions from team.

■ Leader presents alternative actions and agrees to team input.

■ Leader lays out problem areas and gets team input prior to making decision.

■ Leader defines the areas where team members can make decisions.

■ Leader and members of team make decisions together within overall organizational guidelines.

TEAM FREE TO ACT, LEADER RESTRICTED

OUR POSITION ON THE SCALE INFLUENCES YOUR LEADERSHIP STYLE

■ At the top end of the continuum, a command style is more suitable: Your team will do as you ask them.

■ A more inclusive style gives team members more responsibility.

■ At the bottom end of the continuum, give team members clear areas of responsibility and allow upward and downward feedback.

ACTORS THAT INFLUENCE YOUR POSITION ON THE SCALE INCLUDE:

■ Your personality
■ Your values
■ Your confidence in your team members' abilities
■ How secure you are
■ Team members' attitudes
■ Team members' willingness to act within their own area of knowledge
■ Team members' experience
■ Team members' ability to deal with the unknown
■ The nature of the task
■ The organizational setting

Contingency approach

The contingency approach allows you to consider the situation in which you are being asked to lead and how this will affect the leadership style you adopt.

It is suggested that leaders are born and not made, but in a contingency approach it is clear that an individual rises to the challenge of a situation and becomes an effective leader. In other words, the challenge makes her the leader.

The three dimensions that will produce the most effective results are:

1. POSITION POWER

The inherent authority in a position in the organization is often related to the title of the post and the perceived level in the hierarchy. A position in which the holder reports directly to the chief executive, for example, is perceived as a high-level position.

The title of the individual post holder may give clues as to the authority the individual has. This may be defined by the individual's knowledge or power. For example, head of planning, chief chemist, professor of philosophy all define an individual's status.

In such a scenario, you derive your authority—or perceived authority—from the position rather than the power that might come from, for example, your personality or experience. This authority enables you to achieve goals because the team members comply with your directions.

Your team members are compliant because they recognize your authority and respect and acknowledge it.

With a clear and acknowledged position of power within an organization, you can achieve goals and objectives by directing team members who will willingly comply.

The opposite situation, in which leaders do not have this position, may result in failure, with the team members not responding to the instructions and the task not being completed.

The team becomes unmotivated and begins to fail. The spiral of reduced goals and failure starts to become acceptable.

Contingency approach continued

2. TASK STRUCTURE

In a situation in which the task can be clearly articulated and is almost self-evident within the organization it becomes easier for the members of the team to focus and be held accountable for their actions.

For example, a coach might be told to "win the Super Bowl." That clear and unambiguous goal is then what the coach and all his team members focus on.

With a clear task in a situation without ambiguity that might cloud the issue and make decisions questionable and not obvious, the quality of performance will be more easily controlled and the objectives will be easily defined.

In such situations, your leadership style will become less democratic and more authoritarian. This may well be more accepted in the short term, but it will result in difficulties if continued for too long a period.

■ The team members will be more openly accountable for their performance, and failure to meet the perceived norms will become more apparent. In this way with a clearly defined task, the members of the group can be held responsible for their own performance.

■ There is an element of self-regulation and direction. The team will act with more autonomy, and its motivation will come from within.

■ These situations are often defined as crises in which the task becomes swiftly apparent and the need for individuals to act corporately for the good of the organization becomes apparent and is recognized by all team members.

■ The need to "pull together" for the common good is clear for all to see, and will act as a strong influence on all team members.

Contingency approach continued

3. LEADER–MEMBER RELATIONS

Of the three dimensions, this is perhaps the most important factor and the one over which an individual leader has the most control, because position power is based on the structure of the organization that a leader may not be able to alter, and task structure may also be forced on a leader by circumstances. The extent to which a leader can make changes is limited to the relationship between himself and the team.

The relationship between leader and team members affects the willingness of the team to follow the instructions of a leader and relates directly to how much or how little the leader is liked and trusted by the team members.

This also relates to how respected the leader is by the team, but it does not necessarily mean that the leader is easy-going. Often team members want a clear and decisive lead and unambiguous instructions to give them the comfort and security to act.

An organization with good leader–member relations might have share options, for example, as workers buy into the organization's long-term success.

■ The nature of the relationship depends on situation and circumstances. A leader who is highly effective in one situation may be unable to adjust her style to suit alternative situations and will prove less successful in a changed environment.

■ In a situation with a high degree of ambiguity or uncertainty, a task-orientated leader is likely to have greater success because she will be giving the team clear objectives and understanding.

■ In a situation of moderate ambiguity in which the leader's position is less powerful, co-operation and interaction achieve better results.

It is often true that there are situations that are more or less favorable to leaders. When the situation determines the most effective style, a good leader understands and is able to modify her usual style accordingly.

situational analysis & team building

Identifying failures of leadership

There are several ways in which organizations fail, or have the potential to fai
An effective leader knows and understands these scenarios and can work
through them.

IMPROPER PLANNING
A given is that the future is not going to be the same as the past or the present. A leader has to recognize this and plan accordingly. This may be personally or professionally difficult, but getting a team in place that will satisfy future needs and best serve the organization is vital.

Objectives, plans, and external factors (the marketplace, the economic climate) may have changed, but an organization may fail to adapt. In a seller's market, for example, it is vital to produce goods on time and on budget. In a buyer's market, by contrast, meeting the client's precise needs is of overriding importance. A leader who does not appreciate this is going to encounter difficulties.

The human factor is also important. In a new company, employees who share the vision and want to work hard to achieve it are vital. Once the company is off the ground, however, these may not be the most appropriate team leaders. For example, to get your business off the ground, you may need technical innovators. Once your product is successfully launched, however, you may need to rely more heavily on your sales force or on your production engineers to keep goods rolling off the line.

Dispensing with the services of people who have served you well but are not up to the next challenge is difficult but essential to success.

Organizing around people may also lead to the appearance of "holes." If you rely on the strengths of your current managers, are you truly covering all the bases? Most employees play to their strengths, with the result that several people may try to undertake certain functions, while other, key functions are ignored.

Identifying failures of leadership continued

In addition, people change jobs. The team that has grown with you is unlikely to stay with you. People move on: Planning means being prepared for this eventuality. This may be by carefully watching subordinates to see who is promotable or by watching the opposition to see whom you can entice to work for you. Never assume that your loyal team is going to remain your loyal team.

At all times:

■ Be flexible.

■ Undertake new training.

■ Be prepared to meet changing circumstances.

LACK OF CLARITY OVER RELATIONSHIPS

In any group, all the individuals need to know:

■ What they should be doing.

■ How this fits into the "big picture."

Lack of clarity over who does what is responsible for organizational waste (time and money), friction between employees, inefficiency, and constant (unproductive) jockeying for position. To avoid these problems:

■ Set clear goals and objectives.

■ Hold people accountable.

It is not vital (although it is often advisable) for all team members to have a job description. They do, however, need to know:

■ Whom to report to.

■ When to report.

■ What they can do without reference to higher authority.

FAILURE TO DELEGATE AUTHORITY

In a small organization, a manager (or small management team) that makes all decisions centrally may be appropriate. In most businesses, however, delegating authority to make decisions is vital. The disadvantages of not delegating authority are:

■ Decision-making bottlenecks, leading to loss of productivity or inadequate client follow-up.

■ Inappropriate upward referral of minor decisions.

■ Underdevelopment of junior management, which affects succession.

■ Inability of upper management to act effectively because they are bogged down with detail.

Identifying failures of leadership continued

FAILURE TO BALANCE AUTHORITY

The reverse of failure to delegate is too much delegation. It is important that leaders recognize that there is some authority they should not delegate in their ideal of giving managers the authority they merit. In fact some leaders overdelegate, creating a series of managers responsible for largely inconsequential decisions. Leaders must retain:

■ Authority to make decisions that have an impact company-wide.

■ Management of staff performance, objectives, and results.

CONFUSING LINES OF AUTHORITY WITH LINES OF INFORMATION

Information gathering is not the same as decision making, yet in many organizations the two are confused. Managers make decisions, but there is no reason why pertinent information should be hidden from employees.

Opening channels of information reduces problems and costs: Relevant information should be available to all.

GRANTING AUTHORITY WITHOUT RESPONSIBILITY

Any individual given authority to act must be held responsible for the decisions she makes. If she is not, chaos results. Consider, for example, the case of a rogue trader who can lose his company hundreds of thousands of dollars. However, a leader who grants authority to his managers in certain areas must retain overall responsibility for their actions. In other words, whatever the leader thinks of a subordinate's decision (and whatever sanctions he may later take), the leader is ultimately responsible for the poor decision.

The reverse side of this is holding staff responsible for inaction when the ability and authorization to act have not been given. Managers blame a subordinate for something that has not happened, when that individual has not been authorized to make the decision.

MISUSE OF STAFF FUNCTIONS

In the belief that "expert knowledge" is required, senior managers may employ consultants or other specialists to advise or assist. The danger is that a manager may overrely on this advice, to the detriment of his day-to-day managers.

It may also be the case that the day-to-day managers, frustrated by inaction while the "specialists" report, take into their own hands responsibilities that have not been delegated. It is also possible that, pending the report of the specialists, day-to-day activity is curtailed or even stifled.

All of these approaches are detrimental to leadership authority and organizational well-being. To avoid these problems:

■ Establish clearly the functions of those brought in.

■ Limit their authority.

■ Be clear about how they are furthering the overall goals of the organization.

MISUSE OF FUNCTIONAL AUTHORITY

In the ever-changing technological climate, it is all too easy for managers to overrely on technicians and specialists. This, however, is to denigrate the role of line managers. Technical specialists are just that, and they almost certainly do not have the ability or desire to integrate their skills into the overall picture.

A "hiring and firing" policy, for example, in which HR specialists recruit individuals who fit a psychological profile for a position without recourse to a line manager is not furthering organizational goals. The "best fit" personality on paper may not be the most appropriate team member at any given time.

Identifying failures of leadership continued

MULTIPLE SUBORDINATIONS

Most staff will have a line manager who sets their targets, monitors their performance, and in line with both of these, sets and modifies their annual remuneration package. However, this is unlikely to be the whole picture in terms of how an employee sees his role in an organization. Regardless of a line manager's input:

1 HR may dictate when vacation can be scheduled.

2 Purchasing of goods and services may be centralized, perhaps in a different city or country.

3 Contracts may have to follow a prescribed form, with no regard for individual circumstances, or individual manager constraints.

4 The PR department may vet, or indeed insist on making, any press statements.

All of these factors dilute the primary function, which is that subordinates report to and are responsible to their leader.

MISUNDERSTANDING THE FUNCTION OF SERVICE DEPARTMENTS

Service departments are often seen by members of other departments as irrelevant, unnecessary, and, when the real work has to be done, easy to bypass. Conversely, service departments often see themselves as a means, rather than as a means to an end.

A good service department takes some of the tasks that eat into the time people should be devoting to their core tasks and centralizes a function in one place. Bill paying, for example, is often best handled on a company-wide basis.

Identifying failures of leadership continued

A service department should service the efficiency of the whole organization, rather than being a separate entity.

OVERORGANIZATION OR UNDER-ORGANIZATION

When managers forget that the structure of an organization is designed to make people act efficiently, the result is over-organization. It is also easy to overorganize by appointing unnecessary tiers of management (for example, "assistant" or "deputy" managers). Such appointments are really justified only when:

1 A manager is due an extended leave of absence.

2 A subordinate is ripe for promotion and is being tested out in a "midway" position.

3 A leader realizes she does not have the necessary technical competence in an important area, such as IT or production.

Underorganization, while equally harmful, usually results from overdelegation, vague delegation, or delegation to the wrong people.

Team building

Team building and the development of a team spirit, together with a corporate sense of purpose, is one of the most important elements in a leader's toolkit.

WHAT IS AN EFFECTIVE TEAM?
It takes skill to build an effective team. You will need a group of people who can:

■ Solve problems.

■ Present ideas.

■ Communicate.

■ Control workflow.

■ Evaluate data.

■ Offer technical, legal, or financial skills.

■ Get things done.

You need to decide on the composition of your team. Once you have done so, building individuals into a team takes time and skill. You are the person who must make them:

■ Relate to each other.

■ Communicate.

■ Value each other's contributions.

The responsibility for staff development ultimately rests with you. The time that it takes for your team members to acquire new skills will vary, as will the time individuals need off-site on training courses, rather than learning on-site as they go.

You have the strongest influence on your team(s) and should lead by example.

Note: You still need to decide whether the composition is correct for your current needs and to build it into "your" team, rather than that of a predecessor.

It is not always possible to change the team, so working with the people you have and recognizing their strengths and weaknesses will be an essential part of your "recipe" for success.

Team building continued

THERE ARE ESSENTIALLY FOUR STEPS TO BUILDING EFFECTIVE TEAMS

1 PREPARING AND PLANNING
The effective leader identifies the task and establishes clear objectives. Decide on how the objectives can be best achieved: Does it require all of your team or can the task be delegated to one or two who are best equipped to achieve? The leader also needs to decide how much authority must be vested in the team in order for it to succeed.

2 CREATING THE CONDITIONS TO SUCCEED
The leader sets up the appropriate situation for the team by ensuring that the necessary resources are available to complete the task. These resources may be team members, finance, accommodation, or equipment.

3 BUILDING THE TEAM
Having decided that a team is required, the leader needs to create the boundaries within which the team will operate, clarifying the membership of the team, getting commitment, and explaining expected behaviors.

4 PROVIDING ONGOING SUPPORT
Here the objective is not to micromanage (become overinvolved in detail) but to allow space for team members to perform, while maintaining an interest in the team's achievements and monitoring progress. Offer support as required, but be prepared to replace team members who are not able to perform or are unwilling to conform to the agreed norms.

Team building continued

Motivating the team is essential, even if the reward system may not be in your control. The following approaches build effective teams:

■ Make sure all the team members understand the combined purpose and importance of their work.

■ Make sure the team members have discussed and are committed to the overall tasks and objectives of the organization.

■ Each member of the team must understand the contribution that she makes to the performance of other members of the team.

■ Inform the team clearly and regularly of its progress toward the objectives.

■ Keep the team members informed of their performance.

■ Within the team, encourage shared beliefs, values, and rewards.

■ Ensure that blame-free discussion is encouraged within the team.

■ Promote constructive criticism of all members' work practices.

■ Create an atmosphere in which suggestions are encouraged and valued.

■ Team members need to be able to express ideas and their feelings in a mutually trusting climate.

■ Ensure that team members can express feelings without giving or taking offense.

■ Give the team members as much freedom as they can handle to allow them to decide what needs to be done and how to do it.

■ Encourage the team to arrive at decisions by consensus so that individuals do not ignore the best interests of other team members.

■ Deal with and defuse conflicts and jealousy within the team.

■ Champion your team to other parts of the organization.

■ Identify and empower key individuals as "high potentials," or future leaders. This may not involve formal promotion or even recognition, but leaders need "next-in-line" subordinates to support them and lead the team when they themselves cannot.

situational analysis & team building

Celebrating success

No leader gets to be successful without the dedicated efforts of her staff members or constituents. The most successful leaders remember this and celebrate collaboration and achievement.

In an ever-changing business climate, outstanding performance is always the result of a significant team effort. A company-wide culture of celebrating success:

1 Underlines core values.

2 Fosters a spirit of connection and communication.

3 Improves morale.

UCCESS SHOULD BE CELEBRATED CONTINUOUSLY, BUT IN MOST ORGANIZATIONS
HERE ARE MORE FORMAL CHANNELS IN WHICH YOU CAN CELEBRATE SUCCESS:

1 EMAIL OR STAFF BULLETIN BOARDS
You could post your expression of thanks and "well done" by
sending a company-wide email or writing a piece to go on all
bulletin boards, outlining the success, mentioning by name any
especially noteworthy contributions, and offering a positive
view of the future. This approach works well if you have a series
of small but critical projects, targets, or dates that must be met.

2 NEWSLETTER
Many organizations produce a regular staff newsletter in which
the leader can express her thanks to the team. This is also an
excellent forum for welcoming new staff, paying tribute to
those who are departing, adding any company news, and
posting internal vacancies.

Celebrating success continued

3 REGULAR GOAL-ORIENTED EVENTS
This channel covers such celebrations as "Salesman of the month" or "Employee of the month," but it can and should also include people who facilitate the success of others, for example, the people in distribution who make sure sales are fulfilled on time or the people in accounts who make sure that payments are made on time, cutting down on complaints.

4 REGULAR TASK-ORIENTED EVENTS
This might be a celebration when a particular task or phase of a task is completed successfully. Breaking ground on a new building, getting plans approved, or opening a new production line might all be occasions for celebration. Because they are task oriented, such events reinforce that there is a big picture, and that all contributions are valuable and valued.

5 SOCIAL EVENTS
In many companies, it is usual to schedule at least one celebration annually. If you are a multisite organization, you do not have to get everyone together in the same place, but you could make sure that each site celebrates the same day. Ideas might include:

■ Seasonal events such as a celebration around a public holiday.

■ An important organization date such as the day the company was founded or the founder's birthday.

■ An ad hoc event to celebrate a key achievement such as opening a facility on time or winning a contract.

6 PERSONAL VISIBILITY
There is much to be said for what some top executives call "leadership by walking around." This means everybody from the bottom up knows who you are, and, more importantly, you know the name, face, and at least one personal detail about every single person who works for you. You share their personal celebrations, and they share yours. The result is an organizational culture that celebrates success (see also pp. 50–51).

situational analysis & team building

Countering organizational failure

The reverse of celebrating success is acknowledging and attempting to offset organizational failure.

It is a natural human tendency, when times are bad, to want to gather together. This applies as much to the business arena as any other. Bad things happen, and in a good organization, a leader recognizes that people need to come together to share and discuss a bad experience. This might be:

1 The closure of a facility.

2 The breakup of a team.

3 The closure of a department.

4 The layoff of a number of people.

5 The death of a colleague (timely or not, expected or not).

6 The failure of an experiment.

7 The loss of a contract.

8 A failed product launch.

9 An unsuccessful campaign.

10 The retirement of a mentor/grandfather figure.

People need to grieve for what went wrong before they can move on. This enables parting employees, for example, to take away treasured memories rather than bitter ones of an unhappy demise.

Staff development

A commitment to furthering the careers of your team members will give you a loyal and trusting workforce.

Staff development and training make sound business sense. Studies show that organizations that spend more than the national average on staff development enjoy higher levels of employee commitment than those that spend less than average.

Developing your employees' skills increases their contribution to the business, and can bring an immediate return on your investment in them.

Staff development does not mean having your employees constantly off-site on training courses, although most benefit from formal, targeted, and specific training. Competence breeds confidence, so having a staff member undertake a formal training scheme in a certain area (communication, for example, or a particular software package or finance system) does make sense. Staff development is also about:

1

SHARING INFORMATION
This allows your staff members to make decisions based on fact, which in turn leads to effective decision making.

2 DELEGATING POWER
It can be difficult for leaders to do this because they are the people ultimately responsible for a decision and may pay dearly for a poor one taken in their name. However, this is essential to the development of your staff.

3 FOSTERING COMPETENCY
People who believe they can, usually can. It is vital to ensure that your workforce knows that you have confidence in its abilities.

4 FOSTERING ACCOUNTABILITY
When you delegate authority, you also delegate accountability. Your staff members need to know that along with the increased power, they are also responsible for the decisions they make. If you as a leader demonstrate your willingness to be accountable for a poor decision, your staff will, too.

5 ENCOURAGING INITIATIVE
Successful organizations are those in which ideas are the responsibility of everyone and contributions are acknowledged.

situational analysis & team building

Collaboration and trust

In most situations, leaders who are successful will have fostered a collaborative atmosphere among their team members. Collaboration will enable teams to operate effectively in partnership. Leaders need to promote and sustain a sense of mutual reliance and generally a feeling of "we are all in this together."

This collaboration is best achieved by face-to-face discussion and interaction, by setting an example that all others can follow. To achieve a move toward better collaboration, you should carry out an audit to establish the extent to which the climate of the organization is collaborative. Include the following questions in your collaboration audit to get an accurate response:

1 Do people act in a trustworthy and trusting manner?

2 Does the team ask others for help and assistance when needed?

3 Is everyone treated with dignity and respect?

4 Does the team talk openly about its feelings?

5 Do team members listen attentively to the opinion of others?

6 Are the team members able to express their goals clearly?

7 Are people prepared to make personal sacrifices for the greater good of the team?

8 Can team members rely on each other?

9 How prepared are team members to pitch in to help out when others are busy or behind schedule?

Collaboration and trust continued

10 How much credit is given to others for their contributions?

11 Does the team interact on a regular basis?

12 How are relationships treated: as if they will last or as if they are easily disposed of?

13 Are team members regularly introduced to others who can help them succeed?

14 Does information pass easily among team members?

15 Is the team made up of people from diverse backgrounds and interests?

FOSTERING ACCOUNTABILITY

To make effective use of a team and its members, a leader has to ensure that all the members of the team believe in the competence of others and in their abilities to achieve. At the simplest level, this means that each member of the team will take responsibility for her own part of a project.

To achieve this level of accountability, a leader needs to ensure that all members of her team, and the leader herself, are seen to be accountable through a fair system of overviews and reviews.

Your aim is to create an atmosphere in which individuals take responsibility for their own performance and actions and are prepared to report success and failure to you.

■ The process has to start with you: You must be accountable yourself and be seen as accountable.

■ Make it clear that you and they are subject to overseeing and review by others in the management chain.

■ Set and keep regular performance review meetings with individual members of the team.

Developing trust

A leader has to act to develop trust and take the first steps or make the first move. This requires considerable self-confidence on the part of the leader who needs to show a willingness to trust others with information: Team members will then be prepared to overcome their doubts about sharing information.

Showing distrust will result in others hesitating to place their trust in a leader and their colleagues. Therefore it's up to you to set the example and be the first to:

1 Disclose information about yourself and your beliefs.

2 Admit mistakes.

3 Recognize the need for personal improvement.

4 Listen attentively to what others say.

5 Involve interested parties in important meetings.

6 Share information.

7 Acknowledge the contribution of others.

8 Make it clear that you are willing to change your mind.

9 Avoid negative feedback.

10 Use the phrase "we can trust them" and really mean it.

5

motivation & communication

motivation & communication

Enabling others to act

Your ability as a leader to get things done depends on your ability to empower others to act effectively.

1 COMMUNICATE THE VISION
Remind team members why they are there, what your goal is, and how you are going to get there. Do it positively and with enthusiasm. It might be your vision, but these are the people who have bought into it and who are going to make it a reality.

2 KNOW THE SKILL LEVELS AND ASPIRATIONS OF ALL THE INDIVIDUALS INVOLVED
You cannot bring the right team together if you do not know what makes each and every individual tick. Ask questions, remember names, schools their children attend, which team they support. Remember who has studied what. Find out what motivates them. Look at what they do willingly and well: Is there an obvious pride in a job well done or do they enjoy brokering a deal, or handling the media, for example?

3 ARTICULATE YOUR CONFIDENCE IN THE INDIVIDUALS INVOLVED
Once you have put your strongest team together, tell them why this is going to work. If you need to, explain the composition of the team and celebrate the members' achievements:

"I have asked for Stephen to be borrowed from accounts for this project . . . " "Melanie has joined us from XYZ, where she successfully worked on the launch of . . . ."

4 COMMUNICATE YOUR CONFIDENCE THAT PEOPLE CAN ACT AS A TEAM
Based on your assessment of the skills of the individuals involved, you have created an effective team, whose skills intersect. You do not want half a dozen "leaders" acting independently, but six people whose skills—taken together—will get the job done and as a team work more effectively than a group of individuals. Expressing your confidence often that this will happen and is happening is empowering for the individuals concerned.

Enabling others to act continued

5 BE AVAILABLE TO OFFER ADVICE, BUT DON'T MICROMANAGE
This follows from 4: If you have the right team in place, you do not have to—nor should you—interfere on a day-to-day basis. Give team members the autonomy they need to act effectively and with confidence. Trust team members to find solutions to any problems they encounter while reminding them that "my door is always open."

6 ENSURE THAT SUPPORT IS AVAILABLE AND THAT TEAM MEMBERS KNOW WHO TO APPROACH FOR HELP
"Support" is an umbrella term. It could be administrative or IT help, or an outside consultant, or a training course. Foster an environment in which team members who are struggling with anything from a simple spreadsheet to a lengthy analysis of complex data know where to go for help.

7 SCHEDULE REGULAR UPDATES AND STICK TO THEM
It is great for teams to know that they are trusted to deliver,
but it is counterproductive if they believe they are working in a
vacuum or, worse, that they have dropped off the radar. Part of
your planning phase should have included update sessions and
regular reporting dates. Make sure that these are adhered to.
That way, if anything is slipping, everybody knows about it in
time to act to get things back on track.

8 OFFER POSITIVE FEEDBACK
Feedback reinforces your faith in the team. When things are
going well, it reinforces that the shared aspirations are paying
off; if they are sliding, focus on what is good ("It's great the first
quarter profits are up." "Your report into the new project was
very well presented.").

9 MONITOR THE PEOPLE INVOLVED
In addition to feedback, you should also monitor the progress of
the people doing the work. Ask team leaders for feedback on
who is performing effectively and who appears to be
struggling. This may also point out any training needs.

motivation & communication

Fostering collaboration

Competition among employees—and even between businesses—can be divisive. In almost all successful companies, leaders have found that teamwork is the key to motivating people and getting things done.

THERE ARE THREE ESSENTIAL ELEMENTS TO COLLABORATION:

1 Team members accept their interdependence.

2 Team members trust each other.

3 Team members interact freely.

The leader's role is to facilitate these three elements.

CODEPENDENCE
Knowing that success is unlikely unless every single team member works to their highest skill levels is the key to effective collaboration.

WHEN TEAM MEMBERS KNOW THAT THERE IS NO "STAR," BUT THAT THE EFFORTS OF EVERY INDIVIDUAL MUST COME TOGETHER FOR SUCCESS:

1 Members acknowledge that a little "give" by everyone can make a difference.

2 Members know that any success is the result of all their efforts.

3 No individual is always giving while another always takes.

4 Staff turnover is likely to be lower, as more individuals buy into the "long haul."

Fostering collaboration continued

TRUST

Effective collaboration involves trust, being sure that those around you are working for the common good. If employees do not trust leaders or their fellow workers and colleagues, no matter how skilled or competent individual employees are, communication suffers.

IN A CLIMATE IN WHICH EMPLOYEES TRUST THEIR FELLOW TEAM MEMBERS:

1 Team members show a clearer vision of where they are going.

2 Members communicate more freely: They listen and know that their opinions will be listened to with respect.

3 Solutions to problems are more likely to be found.

4 Motivation is likely to be high.

INTERACTION
This is a direct consequence of trust: Where workers know that they are trusted, and trust their fellows, they are likely to interact and communicate more freely.

Although money talks, and speed matters, research suggests that people matter more. The old adage "it isn't what you know but who you know" appears to still be accurate:

1 People are naturally social: We are "programmed" to talk.

2 Shared, articulated goals breed success.

3 Discussing a "problem" with a co-worker may solve it.

4 Communication fosters a sense of common purpose.

What are you communicating?

Communication is the link in an organization that creates a common purpose
Group or team activity is impossible without communication.

In its broadest sense, the purpose of communication in an organization is to effect change (whether from the top down or the bottom up) and influence actions toward the achievement of objectives. Communication is specifically needed to:

1 Establish and disseminate the goals of the organization.

2 Achieve greater sales.

3 Achieve a higher market share.

4 Be preeminent in the industry.

5 Improve customer services.

6 Improve profitability.

7 Develop plans for achievement.

8 Set sales targets.

9 Develop marketing strategy.

10 Analyze the competition.

11 Develop customer care plan.

What are you communicating? continued

12 Implement cost reduction plan.

13 Organize human and other resources in the most effective and efficient way.

14 Develop sales teams.

15 Develop information systems.

16 Improve market research.

17 Improve accounting systems.

18 Select and develop appropriate members of the team for more challenging roles.

19 Analyze core skills of selected team members.

20 Delegate selected tasks to appropriate team members.

21 Lead, direct, motivate, and appraise members of the team.

22 Set out the objectives clearly.

23 Give clear milestones to be achieved.

24 Give regular and supportive feedback.

What are you communicating? continued

25 Control performance.

26 Set up simple timely information systems.

27 Analyze any deviation from agreed upon standards.

28 Implement corrective action.

THE LEADER IS COMMUNICATING:

1 A clear statement of objectives.

2 A logical development of objectives to be achieved.

3 When the objectives are to be achieved.

4 Team members need to feel involved with the setting of objectives.

5 Members should have participated and a consensus been achieved.

6 Teams need to be regularly briefed on progress towards objectives.

COMMUNICATION NEEDS TO BE TWO WAY WITH TEAM MEMBERS ABLE TO:

1 Express their feelings.

2 Voice any negative feelings about how the team is working.

3 Believe that the leader is managing the team successfully.

Why communication fails

There are numerous barriers to ineffective communication. Knowing what they are will help you to eradicate them when communicating your goals.

Communication fails because at some point in the process, the message, which should incorporate the vision, the goal, and the way to achieve it, is not articulated effectively.

YOUR MESSAGE MAY NOT GET ACROSS FOR ANY OF SEVERAL REASONS:

1 Lack of clarity: You are not sure what you are trying to convey, or not sure why you are sending this message at this time.

2 Receiver error: The recipient may lack the technical knowledge to understand your message.

3 Poor or inappropriate presentation: This may be verbally communicating something complex, for example, or including too much technical or financial information in a simple progress report.

4 Personality: A recipient may deliberately "misunderstand" a message if he has no respect for the sender.

5 Disinformation: A sender may have a hidden agenda.

6 Distraction: Reading an email while on the phone may cause one or the other piece of information to be misunderstood.

7 Distortion: The chain of command may be so convoluted that the message is garbled.

8 Poor reporting systems: An organization may not have the appropriate channels of communication to ensure that everyone who needs a piece of information necessarily receives it.

9 Ambiguity: A message may be interpreted differently by two people so that their subsequent actions cause confusion.

motivation & communication

The communication process

Communication is the transfer of a message from a sender to a receiver.

BEFORE YOU COMMUNICATE ANY INFORMATION ASK YOURSELF THE FOLLOWING QUESTIONS:

1 What is the purpose of this communication?

2 What do I want to happen when I send this information?

3 Who is the intended recipient? Is he genuinely the right person?

4 Is the recipient going to do what I want as a result of this communication?

5 Am I communicating everything the recipient needs to know in order to do what I want with this communication?

6 Is my timing right?

7 What is my main point? Am I making it effectively?

8 Have I covered everything clearly? Is there any ambiguity?

9 Are the facts accurate and verifiable?

10 Is the level of detail appropriate?

11 Will the recipient be absolutely clear on the action I require and the time frame for action?

12 What is the best medium for this communication: email, memo, letter, phone call, face-to-face meeting, presentation?

Types of communication

There are two principal ways in which information is sent and received—in writing or verbally. A subelement of verbal communication is nonverbal communication, that is, how your body looks as you speak.

WRITTEN COMMUNICATION
Putting it in writing gives your readers a hard copy to refer back to, and allows individuals in several parts of the organization to be contacted at the same time.

USE WRITTEN COMMUNICATION:

1 To supply information that would take too long to communicate by phone, for example, to everyone who needs to know.

2 To have a permanent record that you communicated the information.

3 When personal contact is not appropriate.

4 To emphasize your views.

WHEN COMMUNICATING IN WRITING:

1 Organize facts and arguments.

2 Present information logically.

3 Don't use a long word when a short one will do.

4 Always consider information overload: In a busy day, a short communication is far more likely to be read than a long one.

Types of communication continued

BECOMING A MORE EFFECTIVE WRITTEN COMMUNICATOR

1 Use positive action words.

2 Number points or paragraphs.

3 Gear length and level to the needs of the recipient(s).

4 Remember that people "scan" rather than read communications.

5 Analyze written communications by other people to work out why they are successful, and borrow from them.

VERBAL COMMUNICATION
Speaking in person or on the telephone is immediate and personal. You are showing respect for the person you are communicating with and may be able to convey your enthusiasm and reinforce your vision. A personal approach is almost always more appropriate when the news is bad.

BECOMING A MORE EFFECTIVE FACE-TO-FACE COMMUNICATOR

1 Know your purpose: Is it social, information gathering, or briefing? If you know what you are trying to elicit from the conversation, you will formulate questions more effectively.

2 Think about the message: What exactly do you want to say?

3 Moderate your speech: Keep your pace even. Pause if you want to emphasize key points.

4 Summarize key points at the end.

See also Public speaking: How effective are you?, pp. 196–197.

Types of communication continued

NONVERBAL COMMUNICATION
Body language, how you sit or stand, the way you hold your head and arms, what your eyes are doing, the many changes in the way you behave while communicating, and many more nonverbal factors, have an impact on the way your message is received. People respond to human gestures, so stretching out your hand, for example, or taking someone's arm, may draw your audience in.

POSITIVE BODY LANGUAGE: CULTIVATE THESE SIGNS IN YOUR DEMEANOR

1 Upright stance or walk
You are confident.

2 Maintaining eye contact and scanning the room
You are genuine and truthful.

3 Open palms
"What you see is what you get."

NEGATIVE BODY LANGUAGE: SIGNS THAT YOU ARE LOSING YOUR AUDIENCE

1
Looking away
The individual is unconvinced by your argument.

2
Drumming fingers
The audience member is bored and disinterested.

3
"Swinging" foot
This is another sign of boredom.

4
Examining wristwatch
You have been speaking for too long.

Public speaking: How effective are you?

The ability to communicate is crucial to effective leadership, yet many leaders are poor at articulating their visions or expressing confidence in others to act.

HOW STRONGLY DO YOU AGREE OR DISAGREE WITH THESE STATEMENTS

▪ I believe communication is the key skill of leadership.

▪ Communication is expressing a complex vision simply.

▪ Public speaking is the most effective way to communicate my vision and enthusiasm.

▪ I prepare my speeches so that I know how long they will last and to be sure that they have rhythm and emphasis.

▪ I maintain eye contact with individuals.

▪ Aggression has no part in an effective argument.

▪ The delivery of a speech is as important as its content.

▪ I do not answer questions if I am unsure of the answer.

▪ I think visual aids help most presentations, and I know how to get the technical support I need to use them effectively.

▪ I constantly scan the audience for signs of incomprehension.

▪ I stick to what is important and don't venture into irrelevancies.

▪ I have the right to speak my mind, but I will also listen to dissent.

If you agree strongly with most or all of these statements, you are likely already an effective public speaker. If you do not, these are the attitudes you need to develop as your career progresses.

It is never too early in your career to improve your public speaking skills. Even organizations with dedicated teams who regularly brief the press rely on their leaders to speak effectively, especially in times of crisis.

AT THE EARLIEST OPPORTUNITY:

1 Take a public speaking course.

2 Attend a presentation workshop.

3 Set yourself up to deliver speeches, as often as you can.

Methods of influence

An understanding of methods of influence or motivation is essential to a leader who wishes to be successful in the management of his team.

You may not be able to influence the financial rewards of your team members, which may be set on an organization-wide basis. However, you may well be able to influence their career advancement, for example, which may have a domino effect on the financial reward system.

Normally you will be looking to influence the individual team members through the design of the job or task you are setting them. The influences will be:

1 Skill variety—the extent that a job or team uses different skills and abilities

2 Task identity—the extent to which a job involves the whole task or a significant portion of it

3 Task continuity—ensuring that individuals can have control over the elements of a job beyond their immediate tasks

4 Task significance—how a piece of work affects the work of other team members and others in the organization

5 Autonomy—how much a job gives individuals freedom and discretion in carrying it out

6 Feedback—the amount of information about performance that is given to the individual

Methods of influence continued

SO TO ACHIEVE INFLUENCE AND ENRICH THE JOB OF THE TEAM MEMBERS
YOU NEED TO:

1 Remove controls.

2 Increase accountability.

3 Create natural work units.

4 Provide direct feedback.

5 Introduce new tasks.

6 Allocate special assignments.

7 Grant additional authority.

8 Allow for mistakes to be corrected by individuals.

9 Give time for feedback and coaching.

10 Monitor the situation, correcting only when necessary.

6

evaluation & maintenance

Making delegation work

No successful leader can do it all alone, no matter how much some leaders believe they can. There is inevitably a limit to the number of people that one individual, however dynamic, can control. To succeed as a leader you must be able to make delegation work for you and the organization.

HERE ARE SOME WAYS:

1 Clearly determine the results you expect from your starting position.

2 Assign a task to an individual or team.

3 Delegate the authority to accomplish this task.

4 Hold accountable the team members responsible for accomplishing the task.

Each task needs a specific, clear delegation, written or unwritten. A written delegation of authority is particularly useful both for the leader giving instruction and for the team member receiving that instruction. It reduces the risks of ambiguity and forms a record that both parties can use to monitor performance.

Delegation is not permanent. As a leader, you have the authority to recover delegated authority. In a failing situation, it is your task to reinvigorate the process by taking back control. Remember the two major advantages of effective delegation:

- It frees you to do more important or strategic tasks (including your own job) more effectively.

- It builds your team members' strengths, grooming them for more challenging roles in the future.

evaluation & maintenance

Evaluating your own performance

It is essential to stand back and monitor your own performance as a delegato

TO ESTABLISH WHETHER, AS THE LEADER IN A GROUP, YOU ARE DELEGATING ENOUGH, YOU COULD ASK YOURSELF:

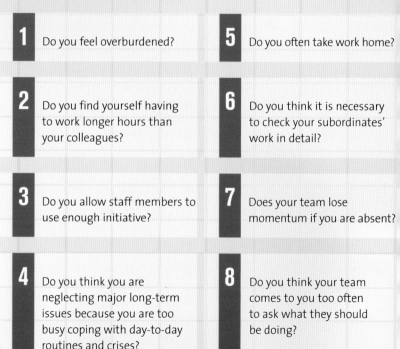

1 Do you feel overburdened?

2 Do you find yourself having to work longer hours than your colleagues?

3 Do you allow staff members to use enough initiative?

4 Do you think you are neglecting major long-term issues because you are too busy coping with day-to-day routines and crises?

5 Do you often take work home?

6 Do you think it is necessary to check your subordinates' work in detail?

7 Does your team lose momentum if you are absent?

8 Do you think your team comes to you too often to ask what they should be doing?

O DELEGATE EFFECTIVELY YOU NEED TO ASK YOURSELF WHAT IN YOUR OWN
MAKEUP IS STOPPING YOU FROM DELEGATING:

1 A lack of receptiveness: How open are you to the ideas from members of
the team. To delegate effectively, you must be able to welcome new
ideas and create the environment in which new ideas can be developed.

2 An inability to let go: How able are you to allow team members to
make decisions? As a leader you will contribute most to the
organization by concentrating on the tasks that further the company
objectives and delegating other tasks to team members.

3 A lack of willingness to allow others to make mistakes. You must allow
those responsible to you to make and learn from mistakes.

4 A lack of willingness to use controls. You cannot delegate authority if
you do not have a systematic approach to feedback and control.

Appraisal, coaching, and promotion

Appraising the performance of individuals and of the team is an essential part of the leader's role in an organization.

THERE ARE FOUR MAIN STAGES IN APPRAISING YOUR TEAM MEMBERS:

1 Review the tasks the team has worked on, allowing the team members to identify those significant factors that have contributed successfully to the task and those factors that have impeded the task.

2 From the successes and failures, select those that are practical to keep and those that the team wishes to dispense with.

3 With the team, agree on its objectives for the next tasks; usually these objectives are concerned with maintaining success.

4 With the team, agree on a code of practice or working method based on those objectives. With individuals, agree on how they are to act or work differently in order to achieve their objectives.

Based on these elements, you should be able to coach those individual members of the team in their specific tasks and develop their abilities and usefulness. You have two main options:

■ Use a directive approach to solve problems for individual team members.

■ Use a client-focused approach in which you let the individual talk it through and develop her own solutions.

The successful outcome of the appraisal process will lead you to think about promoting individuals within the team either to a new position under your authority or in another part of the organization.

Compensation and reward systems

The level to which you as a leader are able to affect the compensation and rewards of your team depends both on the type of organization and the organization's culture.

You will be able to affect a variety of extrinsic rewards, such as salary and fringe benefits like insurance, loans, company cars, subsidized meals, and so on. There are also a number of intrinsic rewards under your control, and studies suggest that these are more highly valued by workers. Intrinsic rewards include:

1 Satisfying work

2 Personal responsibility

3 Autonomy

THE COMPONENTS OF A SATISFYING JOB

1 It makes an identifiable contribution to the team's or organization's end product.

6 There is frequent and adequate feedback about effectiveness and performance.

2 It seems meaningful and worth doing.

7 It is reasonably demanding and challenging.

3 It makes an adequate call on the team members' skills or talents.

8 It allows sufficient contact with colleagues.

4 It provides sufficient variety in tasks or types of activities.

Remember, however, that people are different: There is no "one size fits all" in job satisfaction. Your role includes finding out what motivates every individual who works for you and using that information effectively (see pp. 216–219).

5 It allows team members sufficient freedom to make decisions in doing their work.

Feedback

It is difficult to maintain or improve work performance without feedback.
Because the leader's role is essentially to improve performance and to make a
difference, understanding feedback and mastering a method of giving it is an
important part of the leader's toolkit.

DEFINING A SIMPLE FEEDBACK SYSTEM:

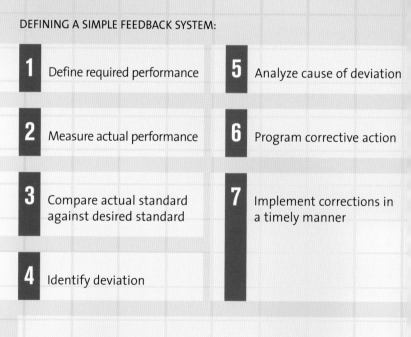

1 Define required performance

2 Measure actual performance

3 Compare actual standard against desired standard

4 Identify deviation

5 Analyze cause of deviation

6 Program corrective action

7 Implement corrections in a timely manner

And then return to step 1.

TO MAKE FEEDBACK WORK EFFECTIVELY, THERE ARE A FEW SIMPLE RULES
YOU SHOULD FOLLOW:

1 Clarify the overall direction and the strategy of the team to achieve its objectives.

5 Listen effectively to the team.

2 Understand the objectives and how the team or individuals are to be measured on their success or failure.

6 Concentrate on priorities of work.

3 Invest time in developing and agreeing upon objectives and standards of performance.

7 Ensure the team manages its time by prioritizing objectives and tasks.

4 Recognize expertise within the team.

8 Manage effectively the work within the team.

Exploiting opportunities

Change is all around us and an effective leader embraces change and exploits the opportunities that it presents. Innovation and adaptability must be part of a leader's style.

AS THE LEADER, YOU WILL HAVE TO:

 1 Interpret change, both outside and inside your organization.

 2 Create certainty and stability for your staff.

 3 Instigate and implement changes you consider essential for your part of the organization.

 4 Encourage a positive outlook among team members.

 5 Contribute to the discussions and decisions concerning the future of your organization.

ixed ideas will not bring prosperity, whereas a flexible outlook will help you to understand and adapt to a changing environment. Develop a personal strategy to:

1 Enable you to assess potential change in order to bring long-term improvements for the company.

2 Give you an advanced feedback of likely reaction to change, particularly the possibility of resistance.

3 Harness the energy of those who support change and win over, or deal with, resistors to change.

N THIS WAY YOU WILL:

1 Learn to deal with change in a positive manner.

3 Gain benefits from the changes you implement.

2 Improve performance.

Keeping teams motivated

Motivational techniques may differ from one person to another so different approaches may be needed for different members of your team.

Researchers have identified three drivers that can be particularly useful to leaders: these are power, affiliation, and achievement.

1 THE NEED FOR POWER

Individuals with a high need for power have a great concern for exercising influence and control. Such individuals seek out positions of leadership; they are frequently good conversationalists although often argumentative; and they might enjoy teaching and public speaking.

2 THE NEED FOR AFFILIATION

Those with a high need for affiliation usually derive pleasure from being loved and tend to avoid the pain of rejection by a social group. As individual team members, they are likely to be concerned with maintaining pleasant social relationships, to enjoy a sense of intimacy and understanding, and to console and help others in trouble. They want to maintain a friendly and interactive environment.

3 THE NEED FOR ACHIEVEMENT

These people have an intense desire for success and an equally intense fear of failure. These members of the team want to be challenged, and set moderately difficult (but not impossible) goals for themselves. They take a realistic approach to risk: They are not likely to be gamblers, but rather they tend to analyze and assess problems. They are likely to be the members of your team you can rely on to get a job done and assume personal responsibility. These people want specific and timely feedback but they tend to be restless and like to run their own show. They will need attention and take up a lot of time; however, they will reward you with good work.

Keeping teams motivated continued

THERE ARE OTHER DRIVERS THAT YOU CAN USE TO MOTIVATE INDIVIDUAL
TEAM MEMBERS:

1 MONEY
This can be in the form of wages, bonuses, stock options,
company-paid insurance health plans, or other items that
reward performance. It can also mean power or status. The
power of monetary reward to motivate depends on the
circumstances of the individual and how much additional
income means.

2 PARTICIPATION
Participation or recognition will lead to a sense of affiliation
and will motivate those individuals who require a sense of
accomplishment and involvement. The leader will need to
involve the team members and draw on their knowledge
and skills. It is essential for the leader to present clearly
the objectives and goals to bring on board those who need
to participate.

3 JOB ENRICHMENT

Making the role of team members challenging and meaningful is the objective of job enrichment. The leader needs to identify those individuals for whom achievement is the motivator and give them the room and goals to achieve. The leader also needs to be sure that these individuals are given timely feedback and kept on course. It will be important to keep these individuals in the big picture so that they are aware of how their work fits into the overall goals of the organization.

The visible leader

A leader who sits in an office and will not take calls will not succeed. Leaders have always had visible signs and symbols of their leadership, such as the crown of a monarch or the headdress of a tribal leader.

A leader must be up at the front of the organization, easily recognizable and identifiable by her followers. The Emperor Napoleon, one of France's most successful leaders, rode a white horse when leading his troops in battle. NASA mission control in Houston had an easily recognizable hierarchy of visible leaders with mission controllers even wearing specific waistcoats to identify with the mission. The need for visibility can sometimes fly in the face of safety: A leader who rides in an open car, or who walks around among the crowds, may be in danger.

In many modern business or political environments, when a leader cannot be seen on a daily basis, she might use the media to keep a high profile and to set the tone of the organization. Daily press briefings, visibility in the wider community, high-profile appointments, and other significant events will help to keep your name and appearance highly visible to your employees and constituents.

One example stands out. After the attack on the World Trade Center in New York the then mayor Rudolph Giuliani was quick to be seen both at ground zero, where the destroyed towers had stood, and on the streets of New York. His high visibility was part of the process of:

- ▦ Showing the world that the streets of the city were still safe.

- ▦ Showing the city he was in control of the situation.

The visible leader continued

IN A BUSINESS SENSE, ON A DAY-TO-DAY BASIS, YOU NEED TO BE VISIBLE AND
PROACTIVE. DEPENDING ON YOUR BUSINESS AND STYLE, YOU MIGHT:

 Set and regularly review objectives.

 Conduct one-on-one reviews.

 Hold team briefings both for the immediate team and as a
process for cascading information both down the organization
and getting information from the members of the organization.

 Schedule regular meetings.

5 Undertake "management by walking about," getting to see all the process of the production facility for example.

6 Visit the "front line."

7 Hold daily review meetings sometimes called "prayer meetings," allowing all members open access to you to express concern and get immediate direction but also to allow you to scrutinize the performance of departments and their leaders.

8 Develop an understanding of the needs of team members.

Role models

Everyone needs a role model to give them alternative views and ideas, as well as to inspire and motivate.

The lives of great men and women have always worked as motivators for leaders.

Role models can come in many shapes and sizes. What they have in common is that they speak to you as an individual and give you an insight into yourself, your values, and your motivators. Understanding these motivators is important in developing and clarifying your own voice, which in turn is essential to your effectiveness as a leader. A role model may be:

■ A historical figure.
■ A giant of industry.
■ A politician.
■ A spiritual leader.
■ A former employer.
■ A teacher or educator.

In the aftermath of the attack on the Twin Towers in New York City, the then mayor Rudolph Giuliani was reading a biography of Winston Churchill, in particular the section dedicated to the London Blitz during the Second World War. The parallels that he could draw from Churchill's struggles and those of the London population to carry on as normal are striking.

Your role model might be a figure:

■ Whose leadership skills you really admire.
■ Whose business acumen you hope to emulate.
■ Whose life and work contribute to your emotional intelligence.
■ Who will help you achieve your own voice.
■ Whose strength under pressure will help you cope with the stresses of being a leader in difficult situations.

■ Whose logistical ability was legendary.
■ Whose intelligence or problem-solving ability stands out.
■ Who was an excellent legislator or advocator.

Your role models may change as you climb the leadership ladder, but it is always likely to be someone whose style is similar to your own.

Networks

Networks, both formal and informal, are a way for you to get backup and support, both to recharge emotionally and to gain information. You probably already have a group of people you have worked with whose opinion you respect or who have taught you different things in the past. What you need to do is to cultivate these people.

WAYS TO DEVELOP YOUR NETWORK:

1 Informal meetings perhaps with specific members of your organization after formal meetings

2 Trade associations

3 Links with colleagues in similar businesses or facilities to pool information

4 Social get-together outside of the working environment

5 Alumni associations

6 Chambers of commerce

7 Attendance at conferences and seminars

8 Lifelong learning opportunities

9 Church or community groups

10 Sporting activities

Monitoring performance

Six sigma is a measurement of performance. Developed in the manufacturing industry in the 1980s, it has now been used effectively in many different business scenarios and can achieve significant gains and savings.

SIX SIGMA RESULTS MAY BE USED TO

Unlike most measures of quality improvement, six sigma aims to prevent defects (a defect is defined as anything a customer might reject) before they happen. Traditionally, measures of quality control fix problems after they have happened but before a product reaches the customer. This wastes time and money.

The six sigma methodology is now being applied to all areas of the business community, including financial services, healthcare, and call centers.

You have to be committed to making it work: It demands top-down commitment.

1 Lower costs.

2 Improve customer satisfaction.

3 Boost efficiency.

4 Increase profits.

5 Simplify complex processes.

HOW DOES IT WORK?
SIX SIGMA USES A METHODOLOGY
KNOWN AS DMAIC:

6 Minimize faults.

7 Build core competencies.

Six sigma requires time, effort, resources, and determination. Most managers act on knowledge or instinct: The focus in six sigma relies on measuring and evaluating data and then drawing up a response to it. People at every level of the organization will have to change the way they work in order to benefit from applying this methodology.

1 Define opportunities

2 Measure performance

3 Analyze opportunity

4 Improve performance

5 Control performance

evaluation & maintenance

Are you stressed?

Monitoring is also personal: Take a life audit, beginning with your stress levels.

1 Do you know the symptoms of stress?

2 Do you skip meals, or pay little attention to your diet?

3 Do you neglect to exercise?

4 Do you regularly skip sleep or have a disturbed night?

5 Do you frequently try to do everything yourself?

6 Do you fail to see the funny side?

7 Do you bottle things up?

8 Do you fail to build relaxation time into your day?

9 Has anyone ever called you a "control freak?"

10 Do you lose your temper often?

11 Do you consider yourself disorganized?

12 Do you have a small circle of friends?

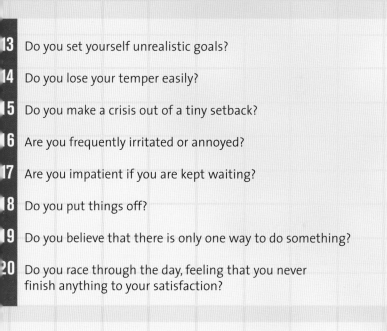

13 Do you set yourself unrealistic goals?

14 Do you lose your temper easily?

15 Do you make a crisis out of a tiny setback?

16 Are you frequently irritated or annoyed?

17 Are you impatient if you are kept waiting?

18 Do you put things off?

19 Do you believe that there is only one way to do something?

20 Do you race through the day, feeling that you never finish anything to your satisfaction?

ANSWERS
If you scored 12 or less, you are not doing too badly;
12-16, you are stressed and should do something about it;
17+, you are seriously stressed and should take action immediately.

Dealing with stress

As a leader, you are likely to be under some degree of stress. The best ways to manage it are to change its source and/or to change your reaction to it.

1 BE AWARE OF WHAT STRESSES YOU
Know the events and circumstances that you find stressful, and know how you react. Does your head ache, for example, or do you feel nauseous? If you can spot signs of stress, you can do something about it.

2 WORK ON WHAT YOU CAN CHANGE
You probably can't eliminate stress, but you can change some things about your day. Can you leave the premises for a time? Or could you learn a new skill that will alleviate some of your stress, such as time management or negotiation?

3 GET THE STRESS INTO PERSPECTIVE
It's tempting to overexaggerate stress, but try to temper your reactions. A mistake is not a disaster. See it as something you can cope with and get over. Don't be paralyzed by "what ifs."

4 BUILD YOUR PHYSICAL RESERVES
A healthy body will go a long way to combatting stress. Eat well; maintain a body weight that is about right for your height; avoid excess caffeine, nicotine, and alcohol; and take regular aerobic exercise. Walking, cycling, and swimming are all good choices. Establish good sleeping habits, and schedule vacation time.

5 BUILD YOUR EMOTIONAL RESERVES
Set your own goals, rather than have them set for you. Develop a supportive network of family and friends, and treat yourself well.

A balanced life

"The buck stops here" was coined for leaders, which is why many crumble under the strain. The most successful are those who manage to integrate their business life into the rest of their life, without letting it take over.

If the company is your own and your family's livelihood depends on it, or if you are at the helm of a high-profile organization, or in politics, for example, it can be difficult to resist the temptation to work all the time. For your emotional health, as well as your business survival, there are some things you should do.

1 EAT WELL
Corporate dinners, meals while traveling, and meals missed altogether will not give you the physical or mental energy you need to match the drive and determination you have to succeed in your work. Taken to excess, they can lead to health problems.

2 GET ENOUGH SLEEP
There are notable examples of leaders who got by on very little sleep. It is also possible to train yourself to manage with less than you are used to, and to train yourself to sleep anytime and anywhere, but your brain and body generally need time to recharge every day.

3 EXERCISE

Exercise invigorates mind and body. It's tempting when there is a desk full of paperwork to skip it, but in truth if your desk is regularly piled high, you are not delegating effectively. In addition, an hour in the gym or pool, on the squash court or golf course, may help you see the solution to a problem that you have been pondering all day.

4 MAKE TIME FOR OTHERS

Families are important; spouses, children, and grandchildren are doubly important. Keep promises to attend family events, even if you are at your desk early the next day. Cultivate a supportive network of friends.

Index

accountability, fostering 163, 167
achievement
    acknowledging 50–1
    need for 34, 217
action, taking 94–5
adaptation, leadership style 56, 130–1
affiliation, need for 216
anger 102
appraisals 208–9
authority
    balance of 142
    delegation of 141–2
    functional 145
    of leader's position 132–3
autonomy
    leader 91
    team members 174, 199

behavior
    self-knowledge 108–9
    separating from individuals 103
body language 194–5
briefing 26–9

career development, team members 19,
    151, 162–3, 209
celebration 156–9
challenges
    and leadership style 132–5
    mounting effective 48–9
change 98–9
    effecting 48–9
    exploiting opportunities 214–15
    perceptions of 49

charisma 21, 82–3
Churchill, Winston 74, 75, 224
client-focused approach 209
co-dependence 176
coaching 60–3, 64, 71, 209
coercive management 56–9
collaboration 50, 164–7, 176–9
command leadership 56–9, 75, 112
commitment, leader's 24
communication 36, 85, 180–5
    briefings 26–9
    failure 186–7
    non-verbal 194–5
    process 188–9
    purpose and benefits of 178, 179, 180–5
    of successes 157–9
    two-way 185
    verbal 196–7
    written 190–2
community, sense of 24–5
compensation 210–11
competency 20, 162, 163
confidence
    leader's 25
    in team members 173
conflict, handling 107
contingency approach 132–5
control
    emotional 75, 102–3
    of team/process 38–9
creativity 88–9
credibility 20–3
crises 58, 135
    acting in 99

decision-making 76–7
crisis leadership 74–7
culture, organizational 19, 122–3, 159

deadlines 31
decision trees 87
decision-making
    ability 86–7
    confusion with information
        gathering 142
    in crisis 76–7
    methods to assist in 86–7
    moral courage and 96–7
    time pressures 93
delegation 163
    effective 204–5
    evaluation of 206
    failure 104–5, 141–3
    under use of 207
democratic leadership 64–7, 112
diet 234
directors 14
DMAIC 229

e-mail communications 157
emotional control 75, 102–3
emotional health 234–5
emotional intelligence 36–7, 59
empathy 36, 60, 106
empowering leader 64–7
empowerment 155, 172–3
enabling, *see* empowerment
evaluation, project 42–3
events, celebration 158–9

exercise 233, 235
expectations 53
experience, past 45, 110–11
experimenting 40–1
"expert knowlege" 144

failure, *see* leadership failure; organization,
    failure of
family 235
feedback 42–3, 175, 199, 212–13
flexibility
    mental 92–3
    of outlook 215
forward thinking 44–5
freedom to operate 130–1
functional authority 145
future, envisioning 44–7

gambling (risk taking) 40–1
goal-oriented events 158
goal-oriented leader 68–71
goals, organizational 12–13
Guiliani, Rudolph 74, 75, 221, 224

health 233, 234–5
"hiring and firing" policy 45
honesty 20, 96
hostility, handling 107
HR departments 145, 146

individuality, encouraging 53
influence, methods of 198–201
information
    communication of 26–9, 188–92

lines of 142
mental handling of 84–5, 92
overload 47, 191
sharing 162, 168, 169
initiative
fostering in others 19, 163
leader's 18, 36, 94
innovative approaches 88–9
inspiration 21
integrity 20, 96
see also moral courage
intelligence, emotional 36–7
interpersonal skills 36

job
influence on individuals 198–9
see also tasks
job enrichment 219
job satisfaction
leader 90–1
team members 35, 211
junior managers
professional knowledge 80
role 15

knowledge
of organization 122–3
professional 80–1
use of "expert" 144

language, company literature 128–9
leader-member relationships 136–7, 140–1
leadership failure 138–49
authority and delegation 141–3
leader-team relationships 140–1
micromanagement 104–5
misuse of staff functions 144–5

multiple subordinations 146–7
over- and under-organization 148–9
planning 138–40
leadership role 14–15, 51
leadership skills
checklist 52–3
leadership styles
adaptation of 56, 130–1
commander 56–9, 75, 112
contingency approach 132–7
crisis leadership 74–7
empowering/democratic 64–7, 112
goal-oriented/pacesetting 68–71
impact on team members 112–13
insight into 114–15
leadership by example 72–3
team leader 60–3
learning 46
from past experience 45, 110–11
self-directed 116–19
line managers 146
listening 46
loyalty 23

management structures 91
media, use of 220
mental flexibility 92–3
micromanagement 104–5, 174
middle managers
leadership role 14
professional knowledge 80
mission statement 24
mistakes
dealing with 52, 207, 232
learning from own 110–11
money (remuneration) 35, 91, 218
moral courage 96–7

motivation
    factors ("drivers") 34–5, 210–11, 216–19
    importance of 34–5
    methods of influence 198–201

Napoleon 220
NASA mission control 220
networks, support 99, 107, 226–7, 233, 235
newsletters 15
9/11 attacks 74, 221, 224
noticeboards 157

objectives, setting 152
opportunities, exploiting 214–15
option appraisal 87
organization (company)
    culture 19, 122–3, 159
    emphasis 124–5
    failure of 73, 160–1
    goals 12–13
    knowledge of 122–9
    literature 128–9
    mission statement 24
    team members' views 126–7
organizing 30–3
    defining tasks 30–1
    over- and under-use of 148–9
    resource allocation 32

pacesetting leader 68–71, 113
participation 218
passion, leader's 24, 45
past experiences 45, 110–11
patience 103
performance
    appraisal 208–9
    monitoring 175, 228–9

planning 16–17, 152
    control 38–9
    failure 138–9
    purpose and process 16–17
plans, monitoring 38–9
power
    of leader's position 132–3
    need for 216
PR departments 146
pragmatism 100–1
"prayer meetings" 223
preference (utility) theory 87
presentations 196–7
prioritization 52
pro-activity 18, 94–5
problem-solving 209
    creativity 88–9
    mental flexibility 92–3
promotion, team members 209
psychological resilience 98–9
public speaking 193, 196–7
purpose, shared 21, 25

receptiveness 207
recognition, individuals 35, 50–1
reflection 110–11
relationships, leader-members 136–7,
    140–1
remuneration, financial 35, 91, 218
reporting 91, 175, 187
resilience, psychological 98–9
resource allocation 32
responsibility, individual 167
restraint 102–3
review meetings, daily 223
reward systems 210–11, 218
risk analysis 86

risk taking 40–1
role models 224–5

self-directed learning 116–19
self-knowledge 108–9, 114–15
senior management
    professional knowledge 80
    role of 14
sensitivity 36, 60, 106
September 11 attacks 74, 221, 224
service departments 146–7
situations, grasp of 84–5
"six sigma" 228–9
sleep 234
social events 159
social skills 106–7
specialists, use of 144–5
staff, *see* team members
strategic knowledge 80
stress 102, 230–5
success, acknowledgment/celebration
    50–1, 156–9
support
    networks 99, 226–7, 233, 235
    of team members 106, 153, 174

tasks
    defining 30–1
    delegation 204–5
    motivation of team members 198–9
    structure and leadership style 134–5
    timeframes 31
team building 32, 150–5
team leader 60–3, 113
team members
    acknowledging contributions 50–1
    appraisals 208–9

briefing 26–9
career development/training 19, 151,
    162–3, 209
changes in 140
collaboration and trust 164–9, 176–9
empowerment 64–7, 155, 172–5
feedback 212–13
leader's knowledge of individuals 111, 172
loyalty 23
motivation 22, 34–5, 154–5, 210–11, 216–19
relationship with leader 136–7, 140–1
support of 106, 153, 174
task structure 134–5
views on organization 126–7
teams, effectiveness 150–1
technical knowledge 80, 81
"think tanks" 95
time pressures 93
timeframes 31
training and development 19, 151, 162–3
trends, spotting 46
"trickle down", initiative 18
trust 19, 47, 164–7, 178
    developing 168–9
    lack of 70

understanding, of situations 84–5
updates 175
utility (preference) theory 87

values, organization 122–3
visibility of leader 159, 220–3
vision, future 44–7, 172
visionary leader 72–3, 113

"walking about", leadership by 159, 223
written communications 190–2